Creativity Across the Primary Curriculum

As we approach the millennium, it is vital to support ways of enabling children to develop the essential skills of creativity that will help them make sense of and take an active part in our rapidly changing world.

Fostering children's creativity means much more than following the guidelines in the National Curriculum or ensuring that the arts are represented in their experience of education. This book draws on empirical research and philosophical thinking from both sides of the Atlantic to explore the nature of the creative mind. The role of play is investigated and distinctions made between play and creativity. It asks what kinds of continuing professional development will nourish teachers. The personal and professional identities of teachers are explored and ways of analysing and describing creative practice are considered. The book looks at the 'bigger picture' in education, asking what sorts of systems need to be designed to develop children's learning in the twenty-first century.

The book will be a resource to teachers, head teachers and advisory staff committed to asking questions, encouraging play and not allowing problems or circumstances to block action. A practical book, it will strike a chord with educators who value teaching within given guidelines but who also wish to teach with originality and scope.

Anna Craft is a Senior Lecturer in Primary Education at The Open University, specialising in professional development courses at Masters level. She is an experienced primary teacher, and has worked in national curriculum development as well as initial and in-service training for teachers in higher education.

Creativity Across the Primary Curriculum

Framing and developing practice

Anna Craft

London and New York

First published 2000 by Routledge
11 New Fetter Lane, London EC4P 4EE

Simultaneously published in the USA and Canada
by Routledge
29 West 35th Street, New York, NY 10001

Routledge is an imprint of the Taylor & Francis Group

© 2000 Anna Craft

Typeset in Goudy by Keystroke, Jacaranda Lodge, Wolverhampton
Printed and bound in Great Britain by St Edmundsbury Press, Bury St Edmunds, Suffolk

British Library Cataloguing in Publication Data
A catalogue record for this book is available from the British Library

Library of Congress Cataloging in Publication Data
Craft, Anna.
    Creativity across the primary curriculum / Anna Craft.
        p.   cm.
    Includes bibliographical references and index.
    1. Creative thinking—Study and teaching—Great Britain.
    I. Title.
    LB1062.C73 ~~1999~~ 2000
        370.15'7—dc21   99–26795

ISBN 0–415–20094–6 (hbk)
ISBN 0–415–20095–4 (pbk)

For Simon and Hugo,
with love

Contents

PART IV
Vision 141

Figures

Acknowledgements

Numerous people have influenced my thinking and the writing of this book – colleagues and friends at The Open University, members of the Creativity in Education Seminar Community (formerly Network) which I founded in 1995, colleagues in Education Now who encouraged me to write my first book on creativity, from which this one has been developed, and colleagues from the former Institute for Creativity. Many of the ideas have also been tried out and refined at various talks I have given and seminars I have led with educators in different parts of the world over several years.

In particular my thanks go to Professor John White, at the Institute of Education, London University, for many conversations about what I have come to call 'little c' creativity during the development of my doctoral study, Professor Howard Gardner at Harvard University and Professor David Feldman at Tufts University for correspondence and discussion about multiple intelligences and 'little c' creativity. Bob Jeffrey at The Open University has helped me chew the cud over many issues in creative teaching and learning. Special thanks also to Coombes First School and Nursery, Wokingham, for their images of creativity across the curriculum.

Closer to home, I owe an enormous debt of gratitude to my parents, Professor Maurice and Alma Craft, for offering me living examples of the concept and for giving me the space, as a child, to find my own way and to learn from my own errors. Having become a parent myself during the writing of this book, I owe a debt of gratitude to Ann Marie Clifford and Kim Rumsey, whose child care help has been both enabling and inspiring. And finally enormous appreciation to my partner Simon and our little boy Hugo. Both have stimulated my thinking, and enabled me, in their distinct ways, to do so whilst, for the majority of the time, on maternity leave. The birth of Hugo during the gestation of this book seems symbolic of its message; we leave this world in the hands of the next generation. As educators, we need to enable them to handle it with care and to engage in it with passion.

Anna Craft
London
January 1999

Introduction

This book was written out of my passionate commitment to foster imagination and creativity in all aspects of children's learning, in the belief that these are ultimately critical for the constructive social development of the world, and for the infinite generative satisfaction of individuals living in it.

It is presented in four parts, representing different levels of and perspectives on creativity.

Part I, Creativity in children and teachers, lays the foundations for the book, introducing the perspectives from which the rest is written. These include a personal framework for creativity involving people, processes and domains and a close look at the nature of play in relation to creativity, since the two are often conflated.

In Chapter 1, I look at the nature of creativity and various definitions, introducing the notion of 'little c' creativity, with possibility thinking at its heart. I propose 'little c' creativity as enabling self-actualisation, and being manifest through a plural view of intelligence. I look at some characteristics of the 'creating mind', introducing a framework for exploring creativity in education.

Chapter 2 provides an unfoldment of some of the principles introduced in Chapter 1, namely the framework for creativity involving people, processes and domains. I do this through the presentation of experiences of two case study children.

Chapter 3 focuses on relationships between creativity and play. I draw a distinction between playful ideas and bodily play and explore how far play and creativity can meaningfully be conflated. Practical implications of these discussions for teaching and learning are explored. Finally I take a look at some of the issues raised by the formal curriculum for the early years as well as older primary children for educators fostering children's creativity through play.

Part II, Creativity across the curriculum, explodes the notion that creativity is associated with the arts alone, working from the underpinning belief that creativity in the sense of possibility thinking is both required and stimulated by all subjects. Throughout Part II, I draw on case studies of children and their teachers. Each chapter includes reference to the current National Curriculum Orders for the subjects concerned, and the extent to which creativity is a part of these.

In Chapter 4, I explore ways in which creativity in the expressive and performing arts enables children to do, analyse and feel, and look at how the arts in general have traditionally enabled the reflection and analysis of many aspects of life. Later in the chapter I examine some ways in which learning in the humanities demands creativity of both children and their teachers.

Chapter 5 focuses on ways in which creativity is central to and may be developed in mathematics and science. Chapter 6 explores aspects of information and communication technology and design and technology. I first challenge the notion that computers cannot be creative, by illustrating a number of ways in which creativity is core to computer-based activities. I go on to look at design and technology and the extent to which design and technology involves genuine, authentic creativity, before going on to consider the social implications of creativity and technology.

Part III, Personal and professional development, examines the perspective of the teacher and teachers' pedagogy. The chapters explore what teachers may need in order to foster creativity in others, as well as what creativity in the classroom may look like.

Chapter 7 is about understanding oneself as an educator and one's own creative potential. I examine aspects of teacher identity and draw on my recent research project which investigated what nourishes the educator in fostering creativity in others. I explore the notion of 'relationship' in teaching and learning and the role of culture in fostering creativity.

In Chapter 8, I look at aspects of fostering creativity in the primary classroom, focusing on conditions for and characteristics of creative teaching and learning, suggesting that in some ways creative teaching is, quite simply, good teaching. Children's perspectives on this are important data for all educators wanting to foster their creativity. I explore aspects of the holistic nature of enabling and manifesting creativity, including the place of the non-conscious and of feelings in classrooms. I acknowledge the need for a discourse to explore, describe and develop creativity across the curriculum in the primary classroom.

Chapter 9 flows out of both of the chapters that precede it, and takes a look at some of the implications for continuing professional development (CPD), of 'reframing' practice in a way which gives a core role to fostering children's creativity. I explore both form and content of CPD. I also consider some of the barriers to such CPD which may be encountered by teachers and schools.

Part IV is titled Vision. As this suggests, in it I look at the practicalities of developing and manifesting 'the big picture' in education, particularly at the turn of the millennium. In this last part of the book I develop the idea of 'little c' creativity as a post-modern virtue, and in social context. The focus moves from the individual learner and teacher out to the systems through which we educate.

Chapter 10 introduces an approach to developing vision for fostering creativity at the level of the system, from the school upward. It involves a look at some of the challenges which may be faced in such 're-visioning'.

Chapter 11 focuses on human creativity as having the potential for both good and evil ends, whilst arguing that education in the twenty-first century needs to foster creative decision making and personal autonomy alongside values of compassion and humanity. In the context of the wider whole, I explore the notion of re-engineering systems and technologies with which we educate.

This book has been inspired by many people, from the very young to those at the other end of the age spectrum. I hope that some of the many learners, teachers and observers with whom I have worked over the years, and who have collectively inspired the writing of this book, may recognise themselves in it. I hope it will provide confirmation for many of the need to foster the creative disposition as we enter a new millennium, and some support in doing so.

Part I

Creativity in children and teachers

1 What is creativity?

In this chapter I introduce the idea of 'possibility' providing the engine for 'little c' creativity. I explore aspects of possibility thinking, such as being imaginative, asking questions and playing. I go on to explore creativity in convergent and divergent thinking and look at creativity as a form of self-actualisation, as well as a plural view of intelligence. I look at some characteristics of the so-called 'creating mind' before introducing a framework for exploring creativity in education involving people, processes and domains.

A definition

The National Advisory Committee on Creative and Cultural Education (1999) describes creativity as 'imaginative activity fashioned so as to produce outcomes that are both original and of value' (p. 29).

The imaginative activity involved in creativity I will explore later in this chapter. But I would like to see creativity as something slightly broader than imaginative activity; at the core of creative activity, I would posit the engine of 'possibility thinking' – and necessary to being creative I would specify insight.

What I am concerned with throughout this book is the kind of creativity which guides choices and route-finding in everyday life, or what I have come to term 'little c' creativity.

Possibility thinking

Picture a time in your own professional life when you have been faced with what seemed like an impossible situation. How did you handle it? Did you find a way around it or did you allow yourself to be blocked by it – or both? Much of the artistry in being a successful teacher involves holding on to the notion of possibility in what may seem to be adverse situations: in other words, of using 'possibility thinking'.

Being imaginative

For me, possibility thinking means refusing to be stumped by circumstances, but being imaginative in order to find a way around a problem or in order to make sense of a puzzle. *Being imaginative* is surrounded by much discussion in the philosophical literature in particular. 'Going beyond the obvious' or 'seeing more than is initially apparent' or interpreting something in a way which is unusual, seem broadly to encompass what many writers mean by being imaginative. When my sister describes her profession, medicine, as 'sharp, straight lines', I consider her to be imaginative. As Morton (1980) has argued, working out what another person's state of mind might be, also involves being imaginative.

Another aspect of being imaginative, I have argued elsewhere (1988), must involve the agent being aware of the unconventionality of what they are doing/thinking. Thus a child drawing a lion in a swimming pool may be unaware of the unconventionality of the representation. Unless the child does have awareness of the originality of the idea, I would not call it being imaginative.

The issue of originality is an important one in 'little c' creativity. Young children's language development is rich with examples of originality. For example, at the age of 5, my sister would declare that she had a 'brown hungry' (for example, a hunger for chocolate) or a 'white hungry' (which might be satisfied with milk), etc. She was making associations between descriptors which for her were original.

A question arises here about to whom something is original. In the examples of the 'brown hungry' etc., my sister was being original in her own terms. She may also have been being original in wider terms. To be imaginative, does something have to be original both for the originator and for the wider world? It seems to me that it must at least be original in the first sense, for the creator, for if being imaginative involves departing from some rule/s or convention/s, the outcome must have some originality in it for the creator.

Thus in a way, finding an original idea or way through something may be a little like learning itself (indeed, Beetlestone 1998 and NACCE 1999 have argued that creativity *is* a form of learning).

It seems to me that being imaginative must also involve a wider originality, because it involves a departure from what is the norm, as discussed above. The spectrum of originality, however, is vast – a child may request spaghetti with apple sauce for a special tea; an original idea for them and a break with convention, thus original in both senses, but not of ground-breaking significance. Toward the other end of the spectrum, a child may write a poem for a competition which is selected for a prize and publication. This again would demonstrate both kinds of originality, but is of a wider significance than the spaghetti and apple sauce example. At the extreme other end of the spectrum are the massive leaps of imagination which change paradigms, which it is rare to find in young children.

Being imaginative must, I suggest, also involve some kind of outcome – for us to be able to say that someone has been/is being imaginative, there must be a public indication of some sort to show for it – a decision, a model, a piece of writing, a behaviour, an idea which can be shared, etc. The outcome of creativity could be described along a spectrum similar to the originality one discussed above. At one end of the outcome spectrum might be outcomes which are within the agent's head – for example, an idea – but not yet shared with others. Somewhere in the middle of the spectrum might be an outcome which is external but not yet disseminated in a wide field – for example, an idea which has been expressed to others, but not scrutinised by the field in which it is generated. At the other end of the spectrum might be an idea which has been turned into some sort of public product which can be scrutinised by the field in which it has been produced. Thus the outcome may not be one which has been publicly debated/explored/acclaimed, but must be in a form where this could happen. The outcomes produced by children could fall anywhere along this 'private–public' spectrum. A child who has thought of (but not yet shared with others) a way of persuading others to care for other children's property in the classroom has produced an outcome at the 'private' end of the spectrum. At the other extreme, a child who has written a poem and submitted it for a national competition and won the prize of having the poem published in a collection of children's work has produced an outcome at the 'public' end of the spectrum.

There are, of course, limits to being imaginative. The person who hears voices in their head may be not imaginative but mad. But the line is a thin one. A friend and colleague of mine is a composer of piano music and lyrics. She hears sounds in her head which she believes to be sent to her, and not of her own making; yet these become her written work which itself suggests lyrics. Her work is ultimately performed and enjoyed by others, both performers and audience. Her work is performed and thus in the public arena. It is scrutinised by others in her field and considered to be original, in that she goes beyond what was there previously, creating both musical and moral dilemmas in what she writes. She, it seems to me, is being imaginative. In contrast, the man who listened to the voice in his head which told him to climb the fence around the lion enclosure in the zoo, and who was then mauled to death, was mad. The musical example illustrates yet another aspect of being imaginative: it does not necessarily involve intention.

Some classroom implications of fostering imagination are:

- teachers stimulating and encouraging non-conventionality, whilst also
- encouraging children to understand the nature of conventions so that when they are being original in either their own or wider terms, they can identify this.

Asking questions

Professor Philip Gammage has suggested that education, rather than focusing on 'answering the question', should emphasise 'questioning the answer'. And possibility thinking is about posing lots of questions. Children enter school doing this naturally and with ease, as Holt has said (1991):

The easily observable fact is that children are passionately eager to make as much sense as they can of the world around them, are extremely good at it, and do as scientists do, by creating knowledge out of experience. Children observe, wonder, find, or make and then test the answers to the questions they ask themselves. When they are not actually prevented from doing these things, they continue to do them and to get better and better at it.

(Holt, 1991: 152)

A characteristic of possibility thinkers, then, is their curiosity. The ability to wonder about the world around them leads a possibility thinker to both find and solve problems. And often, as well as asking questions, a possibility thinker will answer a question with further questions – leading them into new ways of thinking about the world around them.

Asking questions may sometimes be 'unfocused', i.e. a question may not always be consciously posed. Sometimes all that we are aware of is a nagging puzzle, or a niggling feeling that something is not quite straight in our mind. Another way of describing this sort of questioning is a sensitivity to possible problems.

Questions are as important at the end of the process of creating as they are at the outset. Thus, as the outcome of creativity is scrutinised, the creator and others ask to what extent this yield is original and of value. As it is put by the National Advisory Committee cited at the start of this chapter, there are two 'modes' in creative thought: one is the 'imaginative-generative' which brings about outcomes; the other is the 'critical-evaluative' mode which involves scrutiny for originality and value. Both are equally important, as the committee suggests: 'The quality of creative achievement is related to both' (1999: 31).

Some practical implications for teaching and learning of what I have been saying are:

- learning opportunities need to both stimulate and support the posing of questions by children and their teachers;
- the posing of questions may involve puzzling at a fairly non-conscious level as well as actually asking questions;
- we need to remember that children do this naturally, and that much of what we need to do in classrooms involves finding a balance between not inhibiting children's curiosity and managing large numbers and a pre-determined curriculum.

Play and possibilities

An important part of possibility thinking involves playing. According to Hudson (1973), Einstein himself considered 'combinatory play' to be a key part of his own creative thinking. And play forms a part of the six areas of learning (one of which is called 'creative development'), which nursery schools must now provide for children (Ofsted, 1996; SCAA, 1997). Among those who research creativity in the arts there has long been a fascination about the relationship between the child and the artist, as Gardner has documented (1994).

A creative teacher will stimulate and support possibility thinking across the curriculum, in a variety of ways. These will include playing through, for example:

- simulations;
- empathy work;
- storytelling;
- dramatic play;
- role play;
- open-ended scenarios;
- improvisation;
- fantasy modelling;
- puppetry.

Some of these activities will involve a deliberate structuring, and others will involve much less. For example, drama improvisation in pairs, or a simulation, may be set up quite deliberately in a way that free play in the home corner is not. In Chapter 3 I explore a little further some relationships between play and creativity.

It seems to me that the elements I have been discussing – being imaginative, posing questions and play – are all necessary to possibility thinking. In turn, possibility thinking is, I would argue, essential if individuals and communities are to thrive in the uncertainties and fast-shifting social, technological and economic environments of the twenty-first century.

Possibility in divergent and convergent thinking

Back in the 1970s, Hudson (1973) suggested that children who excel in science, maths and technology also do well on traditional IQ tests, where there is just one right answer. Put another way, they are good at convergent thinking, which involves just one solution to the problem. In contrast, those children who are divergent thinkers, finding several possibilities for each question, tend to excel in the arts. Put another way, they are good at thinking of many possible solutions to a problem. Hudson's thesis was that the arts and the sciences demand different kinds of thinking. One implication of his view is that science, maths and technology are uncreative, in that they involve a very focused perspective on possibility thinking.

In this book I take a different view. I would argue that possibility thinking, which is the basis of creativity, is involved in both convergent and divergent thinking – a position which White, philosopher of education, has started to map out (1972) and which can in fact be traced right back to thinkers such as Dewey (Garrison, 1997). Throughout this book I try to show how, for me, possibility thinking is at the core of creativity.

Possibility thinking as the engine of creativity

The Oxford English Dictionary describes creativity as

> 'being imaginative and inventive, bringing into existence, making, originating'
>
> (*Concise Oxford Dictionary*, 9th Edition, 1995)

So the word creativity seems to describe flux, change, development, growth; the approach to life which begins with: 'what if' . . . or 'perhaps if' . . . One way of describing creativity is that its core is one of questioning . . . or that possibility thinking is the 'engine' of creativity. I would include in this the 'puzzling' type of possibility thinking, of which we are not necessarily fully conscious.

Possibility, self-actualisation and being imaginative

There is a sense in which creativity involves making out of nothing. And, of course, there are different theoretical perspectives on this phenomenon. For example, Skinnerian psychology which might describe creativity as simply the revealing of pre-existent ideas, rather than conjuring them up. Or Freudian psychology, which might define creativity as the sublimation of a sexual urge. Or the information processing perspectives which equates the brain to a computer, as discussed by Boden (1992), where creativity is seen as being concerned with imaginative leaps within a set of rules or codes or 'grammars'. As a result of the leaps, the grammars themselves are altered.

There is the psychosynthetic perspective which sees creativity as involving conscious choice over levels of unconscious processes. Or humanistic psychology, based on Maslow's ideas (1971), which sees creativity as self-actualisation and a special talent to boot. I return to Maslow's ideas and humanistic psychology in Chapter 4. These are only some of the perspectives which can be found in one field – psychology. Other fields, such as sociology, philosophy, spirituality and studies in education, yield further approaches to and definitions of creativity.

For example, within the philosophical literature, Elliott's (1975) definition places creativity very close to imagination. He writes that 'Creativity is imagi-nativeness or ingenuity manifested in any valued pursuit' (p. 139). He does not tie the concept of creativity to an end product, but only to a 'pursuit' – in other words, to the process. So, for Elliott, the process by which someone proceeds can be considered to be creative. The processes involved in creativity, for Elliott, are 'problem-solving' and 'making something of an idea'. He claims that 'to proceed imaginatively is . . . to be creative. All creativity is creative (i.e. imaginative thinking)' (p. 147).

Using Elliott's analysis, it appears that imagination and creativity are the same, for it could be argued that problem solving involves imagination, in order to see possibilities. Making something of an idea; finding something valuable in some way in an idea, or having a novel idea, likewise seems similar to another aspect of being imaginative.

Elliott draws an important distinction between two sorts of creativity, the one tied to problem solving, the other not. This, it seems to me, is paralleled in the concept of imaginativeness. For imaginativeness can be tied to solving a problem, but in the same way as Elliott writes 'the value of a novel idea may not lie chiefly in its usefulness for problem-solving' (p. 146), this is sometimes the case too in being imaginative. Thus the value of 10-year-old Jessica's description of maths as 'numbers are colours in my mind' is not necessarily chiefly its usefulness for problem solving. Similarly my sister Naomi's student-days description of her profession, medicine, as 'sharp, straight lines'.

Involved in both problem solving and having novel and valuable ideas, it seems to me, is insight, which is also logically necessary for imagination.

My own approach to creativity draws upon psychosynthesis and humanistic psychology, partly because I think they have particular relevance to classroom teaching. I therefore see creativity as being to do with self-actualisation, and involving choice, which is informed by levels of unconscious processes. I also subscribe to Elliott's perspective introduced above, that creativity is very close to being imaginative, and his suggestion that creativity involves both solving problems and also having novel and valuable ideas.

Possibility thinking, it seems to me, also involves problem finding. Being able to identify a question, a topic for investigation, a puzzle to explore, trying out new options, all involve 'finding' or 'identifying' a problem (using the word problem in a loose way, to mean 'other possibilities').

Summing up so far

I have introduced possibility thinking as a core element in creativity – as its 'engine' – and have suggested that it involves:

- being imaginative;
- posing questions;
- play.

I have suggested possibility thinking (problem solving, thinking about the world in novel and valuable ways, as well as problem finding) is involved in both convergent and divergent thinking. Having discussed briefly some of the perspectives through which creativity can be viewed, I have introduced the notion of creativity as enabling the individual to achieve self-actualisation. This notion comes from the tradition of psychosynthesis and humanistic psychology. I have also discussed the notion of creativity as close to, and encompassing, imagination.

The next part of this chapter examines the notion of creativity yielding outcomes which are of value and original. I will then go on to look at the idea of creativity as 'multiple intelligence'.

Value and use

As indicated at the start of the chapter, the National Advisory Committee on Creative and Cultural Education has recently offered a definition of creativity which involves outcomes which are of value and also original. I would not wish to contest these, merely to flesh them out a little.

To say that an outcome is of value, when talking of the everyday creativity of most individuals, is to say that it has some use in their life, or that it can be held in esteem in an appropriate context. Thus, a child's painting can be said to have value in a different way than the algebraic equation which they invent to predict the outcome of a sequence in a number investigation. One has aesthetic value, the other predictive.

To say that something is original in the context of everyday creativity is not to say that it is necessarily paradigm-shifting in the way that, say, Einstein's work was. Originality implies that something goes beyond existing understandings or formulations. It can be understood, as suggested earlier, along a spectrum, at one end of which may be originality to the learner, and at the other end of which may be a leap of originality so great that it shifts the ways in which a whole field understands a concept or process. The kind of creativity we are most likely to meet in the classroom is the former, i.e. where the outcomes have originality to the learner, rather than shifting paradigms.

Creativity and intelligence

Creativity is not the same as intelligence, in the sense of IQ, as research from the 1970s and 1980s has shown (Wallach, 1971, 1985). Also, we now know that certain kinds of divergent thinking skills can be improved with practice and training. But perhaps the most useful breakthrough in understanding creativity which has occurred in the past twenty years is the idea of creativity as multiple intelligence.

Multiple intelligences

In the mid-1980s, Howard Gardner, a leading researcher exploring creativity at Harvard University, put forward a pluralist theory of mind which aimed to recognise the different cognitive styles and strengths of individuals. He called it the 'theory of multiple intelligences' (1983, 1993a). He suggests that his is a new definition of what it means to be a human being. Socrates said humans are rational animals. Gardner says that human beings are animals which have a range of intelligences, which go beyond those of both other animals and also machines. For example, he suggests that an interesting project might be to apply these intelligences to computers and to see which the computer can possess – and which it cannot; at present a computer cannot have existential intelligence.

Initially, Gardner put forward the following seven intelligences:

1   Linguistic intelligence: facility with language.
2   Logical-mathematical intelligence: ability in logical, mathematical and scientific thinking. Gardner claims that Piaget, the influential developmental psychologist, whilst claiming to be studying the development of all intelligence (including moral development), was in fact studying only the logical-mathematical form – a claim which Piaget would probably not have denied himself.

Gardner also suggests that 'if you do well in language and logic, you should do well in IQ tests and SATs [Standard Assessment Tasks, i.e. national tests in England and Wales for children aged 7 and 11], and you may well get into a prestigious college' (1993a: 8) but then argues that what happens to you once you leave full time education depends on 'the extent to which you possess and use the other intelligences' (p. 8–9). These he initially named as:

3   Spatial intelligence: facility with forming a manoeuvrable and operational mental model of the spatial world. Surgeons, painters, sailors, engineers are all examples of professions involving spatial intelligence.
4   Musical intelligence: facility with music and sound. Performers, composers, conductors, require this kind of intelligence.
5   Bodily-kinaesthetic intelligence: ability in solving problems or creating products using the whole body, or parts of it. Athletes, crafts people and dancers, for example, all utilise bodily-kinaesthetic intelligence.
6   Interpersonal intelligence: ability to understand and relate to other people. Successful politicians, teachers, salespeople all have this kind of intelligence.
7   Intrapersonal intelligence: capacity to understand oneself accurately and to apply that understanding effectively in life.

Toward the end of the 1990s, Gardner began working on a further intelligence or more, referring to the current list of possible intelligences as 'eight and a half intelligences'. He suggests (1996) that naturalist intelligence may be a further one, as may spiritual and existential intelligences, which he is less sure about. By naturalist intelligence, he means capability and expertise in recognising and classifying the flora and fauna of numerous species.

Gardner suggests that whilst we have all eight and a half intelligences we each have them in varying strengths. So it is a theory of individual difference. The mix of strengths comes from birth, values, training, motivation. We can, he suggests, either ignore that, which is what the educational system tends to do, or we can exploit it.

Coming from a psychology rather than an education background, educators looking at theory in the USA have drawn inferences from Gardner's theory about the nature of how schools should be. These were neither right nor wrong, but were a step on from what he had originally intended. Over the past several years, Gardner has tried to make more explicit how he believes the education system can and should make use of multiple intelligence in teaching and learning.

The idea of there being many capabilities of which we each possess different combinations is not new. Nor is Gardner's the only theory. A similar set of nine intelligences has been proposed by Handy, the management guru: factual, analytical, linguistic, spatial, musical, practical, physical, intuitive and inter-personal (1994). And, from the adult learning field, the various different approaches to 'learning style' also acknowledge different cognitive strengths in individuals (for example, Honey and Mumford, 1986).

From the various formulations of multiple intelligence, two points are most relevant for me. First, they represent a notion of intelligence which is at odds with the traditional approach to intelligence as a 'unitary' concept, which is measurable, where individuals' intelligences are deemed as having a 'ceiling' and where achievement from tests which measure intelligence can be shown on a normal distribution graph. I find Gardner's definition of intelligence more helpful: the ability to solve problems or to make things which are valued in at least one culture. He further defines this as a bio-physical potential to do these kinds of things. The potential may or may not get crystallised, depending on what is available within a culture. Gardner's view of intelligence seems to underpin the other multiple intelligence approaches also.

Second, it seems to me that if the process of 'possibility thinking' is at the core of creativity, what Gardner, Handy and Honey and Mumford do is to open up the applications of possibility thinking.

Howard Gardner's notion of multiple intelligences is widely debated, and the theory has its critics, for example White (1998), and in Chapter 2 I look at some of White's criticisms. For now I want to acknowledge the impact of Gardner's theory, part of which has been to broaden what is valued in human capability. It has been seen by many to have implications for the way we teach in schools (although this was not Gardner's intention). Clearly, the emphasis through statutory curriculum and assessment arrangements is on linguistic and logical-mathematical intelligences. But to develop each child's capabilities appropriately, we need to broaden our own awareness of the intelligences in which individual children may be strong. For, in fostering creativity in schools, we need to be more geared toward individuals, their passions and their capabilities.

Summing up on creativity as multiple intelligence

Having explored some aspects of possibility thinking, I have briefly acknowledged the distinction between creativity and 'intelligence' as a global concept. I went on to look at the notion of creativity in education involving the fostering of children's possibility thinking in a variety of domains and forms. In doing so, I have introduced an application of possibility thinking in Howard Gardner's 'multiple intelligence' theory as one highly developed approach.

The next part of this chapter looks at characteristics of the mind which are disposed to possibility thinking, or what I shall call 'the creating mind'.

The creating mind

Many people have written about the core qualities of the creative mind, or what I will call, as Gardner does, 'the creating mind' – a phrase which embodies some of the dynamism and 'flow' involved. In Chapter 2, I will explore some of the 'essentialist' personality and biographical factors which Gardner (1993a) has identified in a range of 'unambiguous cases' of creating minds. But for now, I want to concentrate on some of the characteristics of mature, highly creating minds, as documented by others (MacKinnon, 1962, 1978; Barron, 1969). They suggest that mature, highly creative people:

- think for themselves;
- spend long periods of time seeking to integrate their own thinking with what is outside of them;
- seek to open their minds and those of others to the new;
- seek resolution by sustained 'to-ing and fro-ing' from within to outside themselves.

It seems, then, that both curiosity and sustained openness to integrating thinking with experience are key to successful creators. Many studies have been conducted, mainly in the USA, on characteristics associated with creativity. Examples of some of the most commonly identified traits, collated by Shallcross (1981), are:

openness to experience
independence
self-confidence
willingness to risk
sense of humour or playfulness
enjoyment of experimentation
sensitivity
lack of a feeling of being threatened
personal courage
unconventionality
flexibility
preference for complexity
goal orientation
internal control
originality
self-reliance
persistence

curiosity
vision
self-assertion
acceptance of disorder
motivation
inclination to the off-beat.

(Shallcross, 1981: 10–11)

In addition, Amabile (1983, 1985, 1990) has suggested that intrinsic motivation, in other words, the desire to produce ideas or work for its own sake rather than through some form of external pressure, is characteristic of creative individuals.

Having the inner motivation to create implies that fostering creativity may rest on certain inner mental conditions. Rogers (1970), whose thinking has had a large influence in the arena of counselling and therapy (through his notion of 'person-centred counselling'), identified the three following inner conditions for creativity:

- openness to experience (or, in his words, 'extensionality');
- an internal locus of evaluation (in relation to oneself);
- an ability to toy with elements and concepts (in other words the ability to play).

So, we are gradually building a picture of what the core attributes of a creating mind might look like.

I have already noted that much of the personality trait research and thinking on creativity has taken place in the United States. Much of the literature which is drawn upon in this book is either North American or from the UK. I want to acknowledge the possible 'cultural saturation' of these sources. In other words, what are being described are western concepts of creativity, which are drawn from studies taken in highly developed economies. It is also possible that what is being described is imbued with class-based assumptions. For example, it could be argued that 'goal orientation' and 'internal control', 'self-reliance', 'persistence' from Shallcross's list are all class-related behaviours (i.e. middle class). There may also be other biases within the models presented, which are to do with cultural context. Thus, the literature cited on the creativity phenomenon in any learning situation is only a perspective on 'truth'.

Fairly recent brain research has added another dimension to the creating mind: the notion of right and left brain activity, which may also have some relevance, and this is considered below.

The physical location of logic and intuition

Over the last thirty years, medical research has established that the two hemispheres of the brain appear to take on slightly different roles in the development of our capabilities. Although there has been controversy over the extent to which these roles can be simplified (Cline, 1989), there are nevertheless some deeply illuminative aspects of the research which I will attempt to summarise here.

Each of the two hemispheres of the brain appears to have its own area of specialisation, and processes information in its own way; and, of course, in the normal brain, the hemispheres communicate with one another through the corpus callosum, the mass of nerve fibres which bridges the hemispheres.

For the great majority of the population, it is the left hemisphere which controls logical, linear thinking. This is the side which can compute maths, remembers names, learns to read, memorises. By contrast the other hemisphere is the part of the brain where metaphors are understood, where emotions are felt and where dreams, imageries and fantasy occur. It is thought (Zdenek, 1985) that in western society, which is left-brain dominant, the right hemisphere does not develop as fully as the left, through under-use. Indeed, initially, doctors called the left hemisphere the dominant one. It seems, however, that the left hemisphere is dominant only for the following tasks:

- analytical
- mathematical
- verbal
- linear, and
- literal.

The left hemisphere may, then, be particularly good at 'convergent' thinking – although not exclusively, since, for example, verbal tasks may involve finding many possible solutions to a problem, i.e. 'divergent thinking'. The left hemisphere also controls movement on the opposite side of the body.

By contrast the right brain appears to be dominant for the following kinds of activity:

- metaphoric
- imaginative
- non-verbal
- holistic (non-linear)
- spatial
- musical
- artistic
- emotional
- sexual
- spiritual
- dreams.

Like the left hemisphere, the right hemisphere controls movement on the opposite side of the body. It may be that the right hemisphere is particularly good at supporting divergent thinking – and creativity more widely.

This breakdown of responsibility in the brain appears to hold true for around 95 per cent of the population, including almost all right-handed people. Left-handed people appear to have less clearly defined role definition in the hemispheres. In general the hemispheres work in harmony together, although often the right hemisphere is under-utilised. And it is really this point which is important for education and for fostering creativity. The challenge for teachers is how to find ways of fostering creativity which feed the right brain as well as the left, for all children. Take creative writing for example. Figures 1.1 and 1.2 offer two possible ways of setting up a creative writing task for children in a way which feeds the left and right brain.

The question is to consider how to set up learning activities so that each hemisphere of the brain is stimulated. At times it may be possible to stimulate both hemispheres at once. At other times different learning activities will prioritise one over the other. It is important that all children have access to balanced opportunities.

Autonomy

Throughout this chapter I have referred to aspects of individuality involved in creativity, from differences in style through to variations in the ways that individuals engage with different domains. I have placed a high value on

---

Invent a creature who comes from one of these places:

- A seashell
- The old oak tree in the park
- The crack in the pavement

Write a story about something both unexpected and funny, which happens to your creature on its birthday.

Figure 1.1 An exercise in creativity for the left brain

Invent a creature who lives in one of these places:

(insert pictures of each item listed in Figure 1.1)

It is your creature's birthday and something both unexpected and funny has happened to your creature. Tell the story of what happens, using comic strip format.

Figure 1.2 An exercise in creativity for the right brain

fostering the agency of the individual. In this sense as well as the other aspects highlighted earlier in the chapter, I may be presenting a culturally saturated model, although others who share my cultural context may argue that creativity fundamentally involves more co-development than I have suggested. I explore autonomy further in Chapters 8 and 9.

Summing up on the creating mind

Many characteristics have been identified by researchers as present in the successful possibility thinker, or the successful 'creating mind', and I have introduced some of those identified by MacKinnon, Barron and Shallcross. They involve background attitudes of curiosity and sustained openness to integrating thinking with experience, and include the tendency to display intrinsic motivation to explore and create. Some writers suggest that these aspects of the creating mind imply that creativity is 'dispositional' – in other words, that to be creative, one must be 'disposed' toward it. I would support this argument although I would also argue that creativity can be fostered and developed.

I have touched on Rogers' inner conditions for fostering creativity, which are:

- openness to experience
- internal locus of evaluation, and
- ability to play.

I went on to look at the physical location of possibility thinking in logic and intuition, drawing on recent brain research on left and right brain function.

I have discussed briefly autonomy as an underpinning value in the model I am positing.

In the final part of this chapter I introduce a conceptual framework for exploring creativity.

Creativity as people, processes and domains

My proposed framework for thinking about creativity, involves *people*, *processes* and *domains*. My proposals have some ideas in common with those of Gardner, whose notion of multiple intelligence I examined earlier in this chapter. However, there are some significant differences also. Before I introduce my own framework, I will take a brief look at Gardner's ideas.

Gardner has described (1983, 1993a) as a framework for understanding creativity which involves 'intelligence, domain and field'. Originally formulated by

Csikszentmihalyi (1988) and explored further by Feldman, Csikszentmihalyi and Gardner (1994), the basic idea is that creativity comes from the interactions of three 'nodes': the individual (and their intelligence), the domain and the wider field.

By 'intelligence' Gardner means inherited capabilities of specific kinds. As he puts it: 'intellectual proclivities that are part of our birthright. These intelligences may be thought of in neurobiological terms' (1993a: xx). As described earlier, he has identified 'eight and a half' forms of intelligence.

By 'domain' he means cultural arrangements of disciplines, crafts and other pursuits. Domains are therefore areas of human endeavour and understanding which can also be thought of in an 'impersonal' way as they all involve inter-related knowledge, understanding and skill. Intelligence and domain are not to be confused, Gardner argues, since any domain will require a range of intelligences. As he argues: 'the domain of musical performance requires intelligences beyond the musical (for example, bodily-kinaesthetic intelligence, personal intelligences) just as musical intelligence can be mobilized for domains beyond music in the strictest sense (as in dance or in advertising)' (1993a: xxi).

'Field' is a sociological description, which as Gardner puts it 'includes the people, institutions, award mechanisms, and so forth, that render judgments about the qualities of individual performances' (1993a: xxi).

Creative individuals, according to Gardner, are those who consistently solve problems or create outcomes within a domain, and whose work is considered acceptable by members of a field. And this is where one of the main differences between my framework and Gardner's lies.

For I would argue, along with others such as Cameron (1995) that all individuals are creative, in that creativity is a 'natural' part of life. As Cameron puts it: 'Creativity is the natural order of life. Life is energy: pure creative energy' (1995: 3). Thus in my view all individuals are creative. We all, at a fundamental level, have a capacity for innovation and development. This is part of the human condition. The recognition of the field toward that individual, and the individual's contribution to it, is thus not a key part of creative action in my framework.

Another difference between my framework and Gardner's is that I find his approach lacking holism, in two ways. First, his description of 'intelligences', although helpful in understanding different individuals' strengths, weaknesses and preferences, nevertheless seems to lack the notion of the 'person-as-a-whole'. In other words, it is a very intellectualist approach to capability. Consequently, my proposed framework incorporates Gardner's intelligences within a wider grouping, 'people'.

Gardner's overall framework of intelligence, domain and field also omits some core processes which seem to me central in creating, whatever the domain or intelligences. Therefore I have introduced a third element, which examines some of the *processes* which creativity seems to me to involve. My framework draws on observations of educators at work with children as young as 3 through to adults. I propose it as a possible way of thinking about creativity. As such, it is tentative.

In other words, within (or indeed across) any domain, creativity involves aspects of the person, and also creative processes, some of which are part of the person. Of course, people are often creative in more than one domain.

Summing up Chapter 1

In this chapter, I have introduced:
- some characteristics of possibility thinking, arguing that it is core to being creative;
- the notion of creativity as applied through multiple intelligences;
- some distinguishing features of the creating mind;
- a framework for understanding creativity.

2 Illustrating creativity in children and teachers

In this chapter I examine in a little more depth what the framework of people, processes and domains may involve, using two case study children. This discussion then provides the foundation for the later chapter looking at the nature of creativity in the primary classroom (Chapter 8).

Illustrating the theoretical framework of people, processes and domains

In Chapter 1, I explored both the dictionary definition of creativity and that used by the National Advisory Committee for Creative and Cultural Education, and introduced the idea of creativity as an approach to life. I suggested that, for me, the dictionary definition is incomplete, because some of the core dimensions of creativity are absent from it: people, processes and domains. To illustrate these three elements, I am going to draw on the learning of two children with whom I have worked in inner London: Sabine and Jason.

They live a couple of streets away from each other, close to the Arsenal football stadium in North London. They went to the same state primary school and have been in the same cohort since they were 5. Both are now in their late teens. Jason is an entrepreneurial chef, now in Australia trying to set up his own restaurant. Sabine is studying English and Media Studies at a British university. Here, I am drawing on my perspective on their last year together in primary school.

Jason's reading age at 10 was at least three years below his chronological age, his grasp of maths was very basic and his concentration was very poor. He took little interest in learning at school, read only when made to and would happily spend most of his time in front of the TV or video. Perhaps you could say that he was at that stage in his life the embodiment of the under-achieving child. Sabine, on the other hand, entered the top year of primary school having just completed her first, 2,000 word long, novel. Her command of mathematics was strong and she was confident in dealing with abstract ideas. She was full of curiosity and always impatient to learn the next thing.

Sabine's parents were both professionals, Jason's ran a small local business. One of the things they shared in common was a supportive attitude toward their children's learning and anxiety that their own child achieved his or her potential. Jason and Sabine were united in something else: both felt bored and disconnected with school, and both were becoming difficult and causing a variety of problems for themselves and those around them.

They faced the same future, with its fragmenting communities, unstable markets and rapidly changing workplaces. For Sabine and Jason there would be no certainties, no established precedent for the form of their working lives or guarantee of success in their chosen field. For these two youngsters and their cohort, flexibility, ingenuity and an ability to learn quickly were going to be key for survival.

Sabine and Jason's education seemed, as they entered the last year of primary school, to have let them each down in different ways. In their own ways, both Sabine and Jason seemed to be struggling to reach their full potential in a school which did not engage with them creatively.

I am under no illusion about how difficult and demanding are the conditions under which their class teacher had (and has still) to function. I started my own teaching career in the school which Jason and Sabine attended. I acknowledge, along with other researchers (Woods and Jeffrey, 1996; Halliwell, 1993), that education is, fundamentally, creative. However, I believe that it needs to become much more so, both within *and* outside schools. Education policies such as the reforms brought about in England and Wales since the late 1980s are what I would describe as modernist, i.e. aimed at a structurally fixed, bureaucratic, predictable, world. Their effect has been to circumscribe the system in which teachers operate, and consequently to constrain imagination and leach the creativity from teachers themselves – although the more recent policy changes such as the National Standards for subject leaders, special educational needs co-ordinators and head teachers (TTA, 1998), and the introduction of 'Super Teachers' may arguably leave more room for the artistry of teaching. If I make critical comments in this chapter, however, these are directed at aspects of the current educational system, rather than at individual teachers.

To help get to grips with some of the practicalities of creativity in children and teachers' work together, I will use the framework introduced in Chapter 1, involving people, processes and domains, and will flesh it out a bit further.

People

Creativity involves *people having mastery, or 'agency', over their environment*. It is, in other words, about individuals being able to 'actualise' their choices in their lives, in a way which feeds their identity. But how?

To make sense of this I want to explore several aspects of the 'people' part of creativity. First, I will look at the separation of the 'I' and the 'Me', and the role of choice. Then I will look at the distinction between adaptation and innovation. Third, I will explore 'relationship'. Next I will take a second look at 'intelligence', building on what I discussed in Chapter 1. And, finally, I will look at 'essentialist' personality traits.

I and Me and the role of choice

Here I draw on the psychosynthesis writer, Assagioli (1974). An Italian medical doctor and psychiatrist who practised and wrote in the early and mid-twentieth century, his theory is drawn from clinical observation over many years. He suggests that we can think of ourselves as having two selves: the conscious self, or 'I', which is rationalist and aware, and the deeper one, or 'Me', which we are not conscious of, which is more intuitive, impulsive and emotional. The unconscious 'Me' is more subject to sensation. The conscious 'I' has *choice*, and can 'transcend' or rise above the 'Me', selecting out elements of the 'Me' to emphasise. This idea of 'conscious' and 'unconscious' self was developed by psychoanalytic theorists also, on whom Assagioli drew, such as Jung and Freud. It is also a distinction which some, especially those working on women's perspectives, such as Gilligan (1982, 1986, 1988), might challenge, in that the implication of the multiple self can be that the 'transcendent' self is super-ordinate and more important than the other selves. Nevertheless, for me, the model does describe an important separation between aspects of self, in which one has choice and the other does not.

The key idea of choice has also been developed by Fritz (1943). He describes a contrast between behaving within a 'reactive-responsive orientation' to 'the orientation of the creative' (p. 43). Within the reactive-responsive orientation it is completely impossible for an individual to take charge of their own choices, or to exercise volition. The creative orientation, on the other hand, assumes that chosen results can occur – even if the actualising of them is not clear at the outset. Indeed, as Fritz puts it, 'in the creative orientation, what the creative person creates is something that never existed before' (p. 44). For Fritz, the prediction of the future by invention involves 'structural tension' which is the space between vision and current reality – overcome by concentrating on the vision, on the goal, or on the imagination. Both possibilities exist in all of us. Our transcendent self (the 'I' as Assagioli would describe it) can, however, choose to focus on and emphasise creativity. So we can also think of creativity as involving our transcendent self, making choices.

So, Sabine's 'I', or conscious self, chose to shape some of her dreams and other impulsive and play ideas into a long story which became her first novel. And Jason's 'I' consciously chose to invent recipes and menus, and to experiment with foods. Both chose what Fritz would call the creative orientation, in their area of creative expression. And in doing so, Sabine adapted existing characters in her stories to create a new plot, and Jason abandoned some of the conventional wisdom about food combinations, and innovated. He invented new recipes.

Adaptation and innovation

The examples immediately above from Jason and Sabine, whilst chosen to illustrate how their transcendent selves facilitated their creativity, also illustrate a distinction between adapting and innovating. This important distinction has been explored by Kirton (a researcher in management theory in the UK, who first put forward this idea in the mid-1970s). He stresses, as others such as Gardner (discussed in Chapter 1) have over the last forty years, that creativity is not the same as 'intelligence', and that each individual is capable of being creative. Kirton (1989) suggests that there are two main styles of creative behaviour: adaptation and innovation. These he says are 'stable traits' within people. In other words, individuals tend to adopt one style or another, and find it hard to shift, whatever the context.

Adaptation rests on accepting the existing framework around a problem, and finding a way of responding; it is about 'doing things better'. Innovating, on the other hand, has at its core being able to set aside accepted ways of doing things, and 'doing things differently' – even if there is a short-term impact on efficiency. An innovator often consciously or unwittingly re-constructs the problem in trying to solve it. In schools, and in our education system more widely, we are very good at supporting adaptors and fostering adaptive behaviour. We are far less good at supporting innovators.

Relationship

Creativity inevitably involves 'being in relationship', or in dynamic interaction – with oneself, with other people, with the domain/s, or with all three. In my recent research project (Craft, 1996b), several educators talked of being, as a teacher, in relationship with a subject they were teaching. One described it like this: 'you yourself have a relationship with the subject [you are teaching] . . . so you bring energy in with you . . . creativity is shaping energy . . . I think we associate creativity with the idea of bringing a lot of yourself to it.' In the same study, several others talked of empathising with learners. One said 'it's about responding to where they are at and I think that can be quite creative . . . you pitch in as to where they are coming from, you automatically click into a game of understanding . . . you are trying to stand in their shoes all the time basically . . . '

It seems to me no coincidence that children and their parents often refer to the quality of the relationships between the teacher and the child, and the teacher and their subject, as measures of perceived effectiveness in teaching. Both Sabine and Jason developed a relationship with their own chosen domain, but both had difficulty in making adequate relationships with their school teachers. Luckily, both were able to develop stimulating relationships with educators outside of school (Sabine with her father, and Jason with a local entrepreneur in the food business).

The importance of 'relationship' to learners is well documented, both in terms of relationships between learners and in their relationships with educators (Cullingford, 1991; Delamont and Galton, 1987; Jackson, 1987; Pollard, 1987; Sluckin, 1987). Good educator–learner relationships are key to 'effective' teaching and learning (Cooper and McIntyre, 1996a, 1996b). And as any educator knows, key to fostering learning are positive and dynamic relationships where the teacher remains in control but the focus is on the learner. I call this approach 'teacher-centred but learner-focused' (Craft, 1996b and Craft *et al.*, 1996).

'Relationship' can also involve a need for audience, or sharing the outcomes of creativity with other people, by talking about it, showing it, performing it, demonstrating it and so on. Some people feel a strong need to be witnessed by an audience. Sabine wanted her novel to be read by other people. Jason, too, wanted others to try the fruits of his cooking. Audience was a theme arising for several educators in the research study which I mentioned above. What seems to link them all is a need to know from other people that what they have created has worth – an idea which Gardner (1993b) also writes about – whether it is an idea for arranging the classroom, an in-service session, or a new cake recipe (Craft, 1996b). As noted in Chapter 1, the notion of worth, or 'value', is also identified by the National Advisory Committee on Creative and Cultural Education (1999) as essential to creativity.

Sadly for Jason and Sabine, their experience of school learning was of their teacher planning for and teaching the class as a unit, rather than being able to build relationships with each of the children. I call this the 'teacher-centred and-*class* focused' approach (as opposed to teacher-centred and *learner*-focused). As a consequence of thinking of the children in achievement groupings and also as part of the whole class unit, Sabine's fascination and facility with words and creative writing, and Jason's passion for food and its preparation were, sadly, overlooked.

Yet, paradoxically, many educators find the learners they work with a source of inspiration. These recent comments from primary teachers are not unusual: 'I think the kids keep me going to be honest . . . I enjoy it, I enjoy being with the kids, they give me a buzz' . . . 'the children are the inspiration' (Craft, 1996b). If this is the case, how can the real passions of some children get overlooked in the way Sabine's and Jason's were? Part of the answer may lie in creativity involving people having mastery. Part of the teacher's mastery involves controlling the learning environment. There is a fine line between planning a structure for learning, and enabling children to come at this from their own perspectives. Particularly when, as in many schools, class sizes are large.

Intelligence

As described in Chapter 1, Gardner has developed a 'pluralist' view of the mind (Gardner, 1983, 1993a). As he puts it, the theory recognises 'many different and discrete facets of cognition' (1993a: 6). Gardner also acknowledges, rather like Kirton, that 'people have different cognitive strengths and contrasting cognitive styles' (1993a: 6). Unlike Kirton's two styles though, he proposes that there are an unknown number of basic and separate human capacities of which he has widely enumerated seven and more recently introduced other possibilities. He argues that the purpose of schools should be to develop intelligences appropriately for each individual. As I argued in Chapter 1, adopting a theory of multiple intelligences means accepting as a consequence that schools need to be geared more to the individual.

In Chapter 1, I introduced Gardner's initial seven intelligences: linguistic intelligence (facility with language), logical-mathematical intelligence (ability in logical, mathematical and scientific thinking), spatial intelligence (facility with forming a manoeuvrable and operational mental model of the spatial world), musical intelligence (facility with music and sound), bodily-kinaesthetic intelligence (ability in solving problems or creating products using the whole body, or parts of it), interpersonal intelligence (ability to understand and relate to other people), intrapersonal intelligence (capacity to understand oneself accurately and to apply that understanding effectively in life). I also indicated that he is working on identifying others, such as naturalist intelligence (recognising and classifying flora and fauna).

Gardner has developed a set of criteria for selecting and accepting intelligences (1983), these being:

- potential isolation from brain damage;
- the existence of idiots savants, prodigies and other exceptional individuals;
- an identifiable core operation or set of operations;
- a distinctive developmental history, along with a definable set of expert 'end-of-state' performances;
- an evolutionary history and evolutionary plausibility;
- support from experimental psychological tasks;
- support from psychometric findings;
- susceptibility to encoding in a symbol system.

As indicated in Chapter 1, White (1998), has recently challenged a variety of aspects of these chosen criteria, and, consequently, has raised a range of challenges to the validity of the selection of those specific intelligences identified by Gardner. Since White's challenge has the potential to undermine a highly influential theory of human capability which has reached into the pedagogy and organisation of many schools and school systems world-wide, I will briefly examine here five of the main points in White's argument.

1 IMPORTANCE WITHIN A CULTURE

White suggests that Gardner's criterion that an intelligence must be important within a particular culture is problematic, for he asks, 'Why is linguistic intelligence in, but the ability to recognise faces out?' (p. 6). White's point seems to be that there must be a hierarchy of abilities which are important within a culture, of which ability to recognise faces is a basic, essential one and linguistic intelligence of a higher order. I would challenge this point in that culture in Gardner's terms seems to me to be defined by example, at a different level from 'survival'. Gardner presents culture as a refinement of human interaction, thus validating why linguistic intelligence is selected as an intelligence over recognising faces.

2 DISTINCTIVE DEVELOPMENTAL HISTORY

White notes that Gardner's is a 'developmental' theory and as such is subject to critiques of developmentalism, one of which is that developmental theories give no role to culture. Yet, in my own reading of Gardner's account, culture is indeed given a role in multiple intelligence theory. A second criticism of developmentalism concerns the so-called 'ceiling' on development. White notes that it is unclear what counts as 'maturity' in Gardner's account, which is certainly the case. But does this lack of amplification necessarily undermine the bones of his account? The lack of amplification does, granted, allow Gardner to identify what he personally holds to be socially important in terms of 'end states' in each intelligence, and to offer hand-picked examples of these, which could be challenged. Thus the lack of amplification may enable the identification of examples which are problematic and which reflect Gardner's own values rather than 'objectifiable end states'. It seems to me, however, that the challenge does not invalidate the theory, it simply identifies an aspect which needs tightening.

3 SUSCEPTIBILITY TO BEING ENCODED IN A SYMBOL SYSTEM

White suggests that, due to an over-reliance on Goodman's thinking, Gardner suggests that symbol systems across domains are equivalent, whereas he challenges this assumption, following Scruton (1974). White thus suggests that symbol systems in, for example, art are not equivalent to symbol systems in mathematics, as the encoding of an idea in art cannot be applied in a new context, in the same way that a mathematical symbol can be. Further, White suggests that not all intelligences involve a symbol system – he gives the example of interpersonal intelligence (which I accept) and also the problem of athletics (which I do not – surely the symbols in athletics are to do with the repetitive movements and physical language of each kind of game?). Overall, however, his argument against the criteria is persuasive, as it does suggest, first, a potential arbitrariness in the choice of criteria underpinning Gardner's intelligences and, second, that not all of the intelligences necessarily meet all of the criteria, which seems somewhat to undermine the notion of these being in some way fundamental.

4 APPLICATION OF CRITERIA

White also challenges the way in which Gardner has applied the criteria, noting Gardner's own acknowledgement that the selection is not necessarily systematic, but rather as he puts it 'an artistic judgement' (1983: 63). Gardner has, however, as indicated earlier, in more recent writing (1996) suggested that there may be many more intelligences than the original seven which he identified.

5 OVERALL SELECTION OF CRITERIA

White notes that Gardner gives no explanation for having chosen these criteria. This I accept – and it is potentially a much more serious problem. On the other hand, perhaps what is significant about Gardner's account is that it has opened up discussion about what counts as being intelligent action.

As an attempt to acknowledge the breadth of human capability in a very practical way, many teachers have found Gardner's a useful framework, because it has implications for teaching and learning in schools. Clearly, the emphasis through statutory curriculum and assessment arrangements is on linguistic and logical-mathematical intelligences. But the implication of Gardner's theory is that in order to develop each child's capabilities appropriately, we need to broaden our own awareness of the intelligences in which individual children may be strong, and in which individual children may be weak. Thus, the implication is that in fostering creativity in schools, teachers need to be more geared toward individuals, their passions and their capabilities. The implication of Gardner's theory and also its applications by schools and teachers is that individuals' capacities may be affected by 'nurture' and socialisation. As part of his critique of Gardner, White (1998) has proposed a threefold set of distinctions regarding intelligence, as indicated much earlier in this chapter. One of the consequences of this set of proposals is that only two definitions of intelligence can be affected by nurture; in other words, intelligence as a specific capacity and intelligence as successful application of a specific capacity in a specific instance is, as he puts it 'acquired' (p. 27).

Although Gardner's theory has been criticised, and perhaps weakened, I hope I have indicated in the section above that I do not consider the theory to be, so far, invalidated by these criticisms, merely to be in need of further clarification, even refinement. One area for refinement which has been highlighted through criticisms is the distinction between domain and intelligence. Another is greater clarification of his reasons for choosing the specific criteria which he has selected. Whilst acknowledging the ongoing debate as sketched out above, and indeed accepting some aspects of White's argument, I nevertheless want to highlight Gardner's intelligences as a useful and recent attempt to *broaden* the kinds of intelligence which we value in the education system.

I would like, tentatively, to suggest two more intelligences which might be added to his original seven (or eight) – although these have not been subject to the scrutiny of his (problematic) criteria. These might be 'spiritual intelligence' and 'unconscious intelligence'.

By 'spiritual intelligence', I mean a connection with 'the universal energy' – or the energy of the universe – in a way which we cannot currently explain. I include in this forms of communication which are not verbal, synchronous 'happenings' and awareness which appears to transcend communication channels which we cannot understand easily. Parapsychologists such as Roney-Dougal (1994) devote their studies to trying to understand psychic phenomena such as telepathy (mind-to-mind communication), clairvoyance (obtaining information about, for example, lost objects which no one knows about), pre-cognition (knowing about something that hasn't yet happened) and psychokinesis (affecting things outside of oneself just by thought alone). Roney-Dougal (1994) argues that spiritual awareness forges a link between science and 'magic' and that spirituality is an emerging form which will gradually ascend over other forms of intelligence. Indeed other writers (Redfield, 1994; Billen, 1996) have described the current era as an age of consciousness: spiritual intelligence can be thought of as being a part of this. An example of what I mean by spiritual intelligence comes from my own life. On a recent holiday in Greece with my partner, during a warm, outdoor evening meal, I felt someone come up to me and lean over as if to speak into my ear. I turned around, but there was nobody there. As I turned, I sensed the person handing me something, like a baton, and say 'it's over to you now.' I immediately had a sense that someone had died. Later that evening when I called home to England, I discovered that a community figure of immense importance to me as a teenager and young adult had just died. So powerful was the feeling that he had come to say good-bye, and to hand over something important, that my partner and I named our son, Hugo, after him. And at times when I feel stuck, particularly where conflict may be involved, I reach out to the original Hugo for inspiration. My experience of doing so is that ideas of how to go forward are always forthcoming.

By 'unconscious intelligence' I mean the capacity to access Assagioli's 'Self' (1974) – the unconscious mind, the source of impulses, sensations and feelings, and which is often non-logical. Sabine's writing seemed to draw on unconscious intelligence; she would invent characters and plot lines with the 'flow' and effortlessness of dreams. This idea of 'flow' has been developed by others in writing about being creative (Csikzentmihalyi, 1992; Minkin, 1997). There is an element of the unconscious which some (e.g. Jung) have claimed to be some-how connected to other people – Jung called this the 'collective unconscious'. Some people seem particularly able to access their unconscious, and the so-called collective unconscious (Edwards, 1993; Glouberman, 1989). I propose that accessing unconscious intelligence is a critical aspect of fostering creativity. I explore this further, in Chapter 9, when exploring aspects of professional development relevant to fostering children's creativity. In Chapter 11, I look also at the role of the non-conscious as a part of a holistic framework which may be seen as having something in common with the Romantic movement.

This is not the place for a detailed discussion of to what extent my intelligences may meet Gardner's criteria, as the criteria themselves are subject to debate as discussed. The notion of *multiple facets of the mind*, however, is what I am emphasising here, in that I would argue creativity is not restricted to a narrow set of intellectual activities.

Essentialist personality factors

The final aspects of people and creativity which I want to explore are some of the 'essentialist' personality factors which Gardner (1993b) has identified in a book which focuses on seven great creators (Freud, Einstein, Picasso, Stravinsky, Eliot, Graham and Gandhi), selected for their representation of the seven intelligences. In this study, he identified both differences and similarities between them. There are problems with Gardner's selection, including the inclusion of only one woman, Graham, among the seven. Nevertheless, I think that he identifies a number of aspects of the behaviour of these creative people which provide interesting food for reflection.

One common feature of creativity among the individuals Gardner studied was 'rapid growth, once they had committed themselves to a domain' (p. 364). Another quality was a level of self-absorption and self-promotion in the interests of the work itself. Another similarity was 'the amalgamation of the childlike and the adult like' (p. 365) (something which has been emphasised by others, for example the former CBI Education Foundation (1994) in encouraging creativity and innovation in schools). Gardner noted that each experienced a feeling of being under siege during their 'greatest creative tension' (p. 367).

He also noted social-psychological similarities, for example that love, within the homes in which they each grew up 'seems to have been conditioned on achievement' (p. 367), that each household was quite strict, so that 'ultimately, each of the creators rebelled against control' (p. 367), that each creator had a personal sense of social marginality, which they used 'as a leverage in work' (p. 368) to the extent that 'whenever they risked becoming members of 'the establishment' they would again shift course to attain at least intellectual marginality' (p. 368). He also described the ten-year cycle of creativity experienced by each of these individuals, consisting of initial breakthrough followed by consolidation, succeeded ten years later by a subsequent breakthrough which was more integrative, and so on and so on. He indicates that each of these creators was 'productive each day' (p. 372), and that in the nature of their creativity, each demonstrated the capacity to identify and then explore 'asynchrony' with others within their field of endeavour. Breaking away from an established wisdom is in his view an essential aspect of the creative process as demonstrated by these seven individuals.

Gardner's study, as he himself recognises, is based on a narrow group of individuals, mainly men, from a particular period of history and all of whom were remarkable. However, I find the notion of identifying key qualities in their creativity useful, even when focusing on the ordinary rather than the extraordinary. Indeed, some of the 'essentialist' characteristics (childlike qualities, feeling under siege, being on the edge, high energy and productivity) which Gardner identifies appeared among educators in the research project I undertook from 1995–96 (Craft, 1996b). So, we might expect to see some of the qualities described above in ordinary individuals: the childlike playfulness, the feeling of being under siege whilst being creative, the connection between love and achievement, the wish to be 'on the edge', high energy and productivity, and so on. And, of course, it could be that each kind of creativity involves different personal responses. As a parent or a teacher the feeling of being under siege, for example, is very common!

To return to Sabine and Jason, the latter certainly demonstrated childlike playfulness in his inventions, and rebelled against his parents' wishes to encourage him to be a more active child (he preferred sedentary occupations such as watching TV/videos or enjoying a good meal, and therefore was rather a heavy child, which his parents tried to 'manage' by providing him with an expensive bike, and various physical activities). He used leverage in rebelling against his parents, offering to invent and prepare family meals, trying to do some form of food creation each day, which then resulted in parental approval (and gratitude!).

Sabine also wrote every day that she could. On a day when she could not because of family events, she felt frustrated. During a writing session, particularly as a story unfolded, and when she felt 'on a roll' with her creativity, she would feel under siege from her mum to tidy her room, or from her siblings wanting her to come and play. She, too, sought parental approval (particularly her father's), for her writing. She exhibited high energy around her writing.

I want to turn now to the second aspect of the framework: processes.

Processes

Over the years there have been many definitions of the interwoven processes involved in creativity. I want to focus on some drawn from recent research (Craft, 1996b; Craft *et al.*, 1996; Fryer and Collings, 1991; Fryer, 1996; Shagoury Hubbard, 1996). These are summarised in Figure 2.1, which has as the source, 'impulse', and which flows through different levels of creative source and expression to 'creativity as an approach to life'. Think of it as similar to a geographic diagram of a slice through the earth, showing all the soil layers and sediments.

CREATIVITY AS AN APPROACH TO LIFE

↑

RISK-TAKING, AND THE CREATIVITY CYCLE

↑

BEING IMAGINATIVE: PROBLEM FINDING/SOLVING, THINKING,

↑

THE UNCONSCIOUS, INTUITIVE, SPIRITUAL AND EMOTIONAL

↑

IMPULSE (the bedrock and source of creativity)

Figure 2.1 Creativity processes

The bedrock of impulse feeds the unconscious, intuitive, spiritual and emotional

The sources of creativity are not always conscious or rational. At times we may not be aware that the creative impulse involves thinking at all. The intuitive, spiritual and emotional also feed creativity – fed themselves by the bedrock of impulse. Here are two examples.

One of Sabine's main characters, featuring in many of her stories, emerged out of her imaginative play, when she was 3. She created Bong and Petit, who were invisible and loved to create mischief. They had a way, however, of knowing what might need to be done in any given situation, to help someone out or to understand a process which might be going on. Like many children's imaginary friends, Bong and Petit 'lived' with Sabine in her day-to-day life, and featured in her stories.

My second example comes from an educator participating in one of my recent research projects. She woke up in the middle of the night with a new melody playing in her head. She hurried downstairs to the piano, and played it out. It eventually became the core theme to an end-of-term opera (Craft, 1996b). In both cases the creators found their creations 'came to them' without their being conscious of them, and they were able to develop them intuitively. In both cases the creators were emotionally and spiritually entangled with their creation.

Sometimes, we are unable to articulate to ourselves what we know or can do – in which case we undergo experiences in a state of 'not-knowing' until a meaningful pattern emerges (Salzberger-Wittenberg *et al.*, 1983). When Jason, for example, is creating new recipes, he gets stuck for a few days and then suddenly it comes to him. His unconscious 'Self' is working on solutions to the problem, from which his conscious 'I' then selects an answer.

Being imaginative: problem finding/solving, and thinking

As I discussed in Chapter 1, creativity involves *using one's imagination* in any given situation: not being satisfied with what already exists, but considering other possibilities, which may include ones we do not yet know about. So, creativity also involves having original ideas, which can come from seeing connections between two or more seemingly unrelated things.

As the American researcher, Csikszentmihalyi, has said (1992, 1996), creativity is about both problem solving and problem finding. In other words, the formulation of a problem is just as important a part of creativity as the solving of one – as I suggested in relation to possibility thinking in Chapter 1. Here is an example from Jason. When I asked Jason to think of a starter for my dinner party, I was inviting him to solve a problem which I had selected – Cziksentmihalyi calls this a 'presented' problem. But on lots of other occasions he found problems to solve of his own accord. For example, at the end of the last school year, his teacher left his school to move on to a new teaching post. His cohort of classmates decided to create a surprise party for her, and during playtimes several children organised the making of a tape of her favourite music, and a short cabaret. Another child co-ordinated the making of cards for the teacher. It was Jason who realised that nobody had thought about refreshments, and called this to the attention of the whole group. He had, therefore, identified a problem. He then went on to define it into much smaller elements which could be tackled. Led by Jason, the children worked out what they would like to have and how to get it. They reprographed a note to parents co-written by Jason and the head teacher requesting small food donations from parents. As a consequence a feast was collected. Jason then co-ordinated the presentation of what had come in, with a small band of volunteers, so that eventually a beautifully laid out party table had been created as a wonderful surprise for their teacher. This is an example of problem finding, followed by problem definition.

I suggested in Chapter 1 that creativity involves *divergent thinking* (what de Bono has called 'parallel thinking' (1995), i.e. thinking from 'what if', association, intuition and possibility; beginning from questions – why? how else? instead of thinking in a linear fashion). But creativity also involves *convergent thinking*, or finding possibilities which fit a set of needs; this is how the end-stage of problem solving is completed. The same creative act may involve both divergent and convergent thinking. Take Jason's task of thinking up a good starter for a dinner party I was planning. He checked what kinds of food my guests might and might not eat, and also what the rest of the meal was to be. A week or so later, he invented a new idea using cracked wheat and chopped fruit. To do this he used 'what if', or divergent thinking, finding combinations of foods which seemed initially unrelated. But he also used convergent thinking: his idea had to fit in with the identified needs.

Risk-taking and the creativity cycle

Being able and willing to have a go at expressing oneself is essential to creativity. Thus, it can involve taking risks and being witnessed doing so. In their different ways, both Jason and Sabine took risks (Jason with unusual food combinations, and Sabine with putting her personal friends into her stories) and were witnessed (each, initially by their families and later by a wider audience).

Creativity involves a cycle. The *creativity cycle* is often described as having five stages (Figure 2.2). I will illustrate what I mean by these five stages by drawing on Sabine and, for the very last part, Jason.

First, is 'preparation' – getting into an appropriate 'place' for being creative. What this means is very personal. It can mean a physical space, also an emotional space, it can mean making time, or being with other people who stimulate or support or both. Preparation can also mean reaching a point of frustration with an issue where one feels the need to make change happen. For Sabine, that was being at home, in a quiet corner of the kitchen, with her colouring pens, writing materials and sometimes clay for modelling. She liked to know someone was around, usually her dad, with whom she could check out ideas. She also liked to draw pictures and make clay models of some of the situations which her

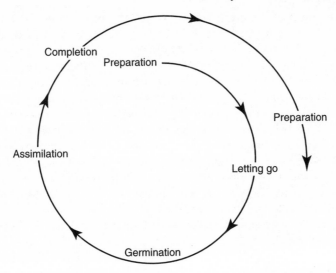

Figure 2.2 The creativity cycle

characters experienced in her stories. Sometimes she would feel terribly stuck and get quite bad tempered before she could progress. I certainly know that feeling when I am writing!

Then, there is 'letting go'. In other words, a period of passivity, emptiness, lack of direction and loss, where the main activity is about letting go and surrendering control. For Sabine this was where her colouring pens and modelling clay would come in. Drawing or modelling the characters and situations was a way of letting her unconscious self give her ideas. It is not dissimilar to playing, about more of which in Chapter 3.

Letting go is followed by what Robert Fritz (1943) has called 'germination' (when the idea is conceived, often accompanied by a great burst of energy), during which 'excitement, interest and freshness abound . . . there can be great insight, realisation, enthusiasm, change, and a sense of power' (p. 82). When Sabine was at this point she would chatter aloud, to her characters and to her dad, and would write furiously, and as fast as she could. It could be difficult to get her to stop for dinner, or for her swimming and recorder lessons.

The period of germination is followed by assimilation, like the gestation period of the human birth cycle. It is the least visible, and is an internal stage, which requires time to take root. For Sabine this would often take place on her walk to school, on the swings in the park, when playing with friends, at her drama group. She would gradually finalise ideas without really knowing how it happened.

The last stage, completion, involves the bringing to fruition of the idea which involves the capacity to 'receive' as well as to 'create'. Fritz likens it to giving birth. For Sabine this was when she put the story on to the computer and edited it to be just how she wanted it.

A final aspect of the creative cycle is that *creativity increases and multiplies*. Creativity leads to more creativity. Thus the cycle begins again, only this time there is more than one cycle generated by the previous one. Having invented one starter, Jason then went on to compile a whole series of them, getting permission to prepare them for his family in addition to the main course during the half term week – a different one every other night. And he began to wonder about catering the starters for my dinner parties. He also began to wonder about going to catering school (which in fact he did, eventually, do). Sabine's first novel led on to another, with some of the same characters in it. She also made copies of the first one, and bound them. She circulated them to children who were interested in reading stories written by children, which led to the idea of starting a club, which she did. She also wrote a play based on the first novel, which the club performed to parents and interested others.

Of course, the process of creativity varies from person to person. Some people need a lot of time in the preparation stage, others get 'stuck' in the 'letting go' phase, others are very focused on the 'completion' stage and consequently have perhaps a more 'goals-oriented' approach to their own creativity. Individuals have their own strengths and weaknesses in engaging with the processes of the creativity cycle. And there is no 'right way' of being creative.

In February 1998, the National Advisory Committee on Creative and Cultural Education was set up by the Secretary of State for Education in England and Wales. I referred to its report in Chapter 1. The Committee's role included making recommendations on the creative development of young people through formal and informal education. As part of the debate around that process, Abbott has argued that being creative is a skill which needs practice (Abbott, 1998). With practice, individuals develop what he calls 'expertise' in creativity. I, too, subscribe to this view, although Abbott's conception of creativity seems to be mainly about solving, rather than also finding, problems.

So, from the creative impulse, through its forms of expression, I have suggested that creativity can be shaped, crafted and encouraged. What I am describing is *creativity as an approach to life*. It may involve solving problems, but it is not exclusively about this. It is not exclusively about performance, or about thinking, or about painting, or about scientific method, or about algebra, or about dramatic play. It is about having one's approach to life in 'possibility mode' or 'what if' mode, in any domain.

Domains

A domain can be understood in a variety of ways. The way I am using the term is to describe a body of organised knowledge about a specific topic. By 'domain' I do not necessarily mean a subject area, for example 'the English language', as this is too big. But verbal communication, or 'speaking and listening' as it is described in the National Curriculum, would be a domain, as would 'literature appreciation'. They are distinct enough to be reasonably separate from one another, and yet to be recognised as both forming elements of the cluster of knowledge which we call 'the English language'.

Domains generally exist before a person contributes to or transforms them (although new domains have started throughout history; for example, social geography, electronic information exchange via computers and phone lines). Domains have a history which can be studied. Usually, domains are described through specially developed symbolic representation (for example, words, music, algebraic algorithms, etc.). The more that a person knows about a domain, the more they are able to evaluate the extent to which a new contribution to it is in fact creative (i.e. different).

Obviously, creativity looks different in each domain, because each one involves different core concepts and behaviours. Thus creativity in arithmetic could mean finding more than one way of solving a numerical problem, demonstrated using deductive reasoning (i.e. 'if this happens then that will follow') and expressed in mathematical symbols. Creativity in social and personal interaction, on the other hand, could mean inventing a new game, or form of social gathering, using 'inductive reasoning' ('this kind of idea has worked in the past, so I'll expect it to again') and expressed in spoken or written words.

Creativity within each domain will change over time. So, for example, the invention of the skateboard was a creative development of roller skates; the creation of roller blades is a development again of both. The ways in which children and adults use skateboards and roller blades developed very quickly after their invention, through creative play in various parts of the world. The inventions include fashionable acrobatics and dancing as well as simply travelling fast!

Although creativity will look different in each domain, there are common features, such as the manifestation of some kind of transformation, through being open to lots of possibilities. Playfulness and being willing to have a go are also features, as is *choosing* to express and apply our ideas.

My main reason for suggesting domains as part of the framework for thinking about creativity is that the notion of domains gets us away from thinking that creativity is just about the arts. Creativity is about *all* knowledge. And this approach to creativity is also shared by others, for example Abbott, whose views on developing expertise in creativity I introduced above (Abbott, 1998). Considering the many domains of creativity also reminds us that the personal and process aspects of creativity are only a part of the picture, and not the whole of it.

Take Jason and Sabine. In the examples I have given here, they demonstrated creative action in different domains. Sabine in writing, Jason in the preparation of food. The examples reflect their strengths and interests at the time that I first met them. Gardner suggests that each of us may have biologically different levels of capability for using different 'intelligences'. Thus, for example, Sabine seems to have a biologically determined capability at linguistic and logical mathematical intelligences in particular.

Gardner's work on multiple intelligences appears to relate intelligences to domains of application. Thus, logical-mathematical intelligence may be seen as 'played out' in the sciences and in mathematics. However, I would want to argue that the domain is distinct from the intelligence. Domains are those in which socially organised and specialist activity take place. They involve peer recognition and a critical mass in order to exist. Intelligence on the other hand may be seen as a property of individuals, and involves their potential to perform in a domain, drawing on heritable traits. Thus, I would see intelligence as a feature of the 'people' side of the prism and domains as a distinct concept.

The creativity framework as an interpretive prism

There is an advertisement shown in British cinemas for some kind of alcoholic drink in which a guest at a wedding looks at aspects of the celebration through the bottle of spirit, which distorts the picture in amusing ways. I consider the practical framework for describing creativity as being rather similar, although hopefully less distorting! It is like a prism which enables us to split out three elements in each creative act: people, process, domain.

The prism is three-dimensional, and I visualise it to be rather like three overlapping cones. Several colleagues with whom I have shared this model have suggested other possible metaphors for describing creativity – one being a crystal, which grows. I find this image compelling, in that it has the potential to split and represent reality in many different facets. I have retained my prism, however, as this maintains the integrity of the three aspects which form the framework – people, processes and domains – whilst also incorporating the notion of being able to see different reflections and refractions of reality.

Sabine's experience of personal and process aspects of creativity in the domain of creative writing were positive, although what her school contributed left a lot to be desired. Using the framework we can see she needed more stimulation in relationship with an educator in school, but was very confident in the process of creating, through which she was able to let her intuitive, unconscious self be expressed. The framework might also lead us to ask how far Sabine was experiencing creativity in other domains.

The framework enables us to see that Jason, too, lacked adequate relationships with educators in school. And that he was particularly good at taking risks, and using both divergent and convergent thinking. Again, we might ask how far Jason might be able to experience creativity in other domains.

As to the problem of how to provide stimulating relationships for each, some writers in this field (Fryer, 1996; Shagoury Hubbard, 1996; Torrance, 1984) advocate mentoring. All of these writers have recommended the key role of teachers and/or other adults as mentor (on a one-to-one basis) in supporting the development and expression of pupils' creativity. Shagoury Hubbard (1996) also talks about children taking on the mentor role where appropriate.

Mentoring enables someone with greater expertise to help someone with less expertise in any given domain. It is a similar idea to Vygotsky's notion of an expert 'scaffolding' the learning of a novice. Mentoring creativity means providing a role-model, as well as direct support, for the learner. In other words, mentoring is one of the strategies which brings together the three aspects of creativity, the person, the process and the domain.

What does creativity look like in the primary classroom?

Creativity in the primary classroom will, of course, involve the same elements: people – many aspects of the children and their teacher; processes, as discussed above; and the domains of learning which are on offer. In Chapter 8, I examine some other aspects of fostering creativity in the classroom: physical and conceptual space in which to create, the artistry of good teaching and what children can tell us.

In the discussion of processes, I have made reference to some non-conscious aspects of creating. The non-conscious is just one element of the 'whole'.

Summing up

I have explored the framework of people, processes and domains a little further, using the case studies of two children to illustrate them. I have discussed the following aspects of the 'people' part of the framework:

- the separation of the 'I' and the 'Me', and the role of choice;
- the distinction between adaptation and innovation;
- 'relationship' as essential to creativity;
- intelligence: I have suggested two possible further intelligences – 'spiritual intelligence' and 'unconscious intelligence';
- 'essentialist' personality traits found in creative individuals.

I have explored several interwoven processes of creativity:

- the bedrock of impulse;
- the unconscious, intuitive, spiritual and emotional which it feeds;
- being imaginative: problem finding/solving, thinking, which these in turn feed;
- risk-taking, and the creativity cycle, which these in turn feed, ultimately supporting creativity as a way of life.

Third, I have discussed domains as the medium in which a person is creative.

Finally, I have looked at how the framework as a whole might help us to interpret the creative experiences (or lack of them) for individual learners in classrooms, suggesting that in fostering relationship as an aspect of creativity, mentoring by both children and adults can form an important aspect of a creative classroom.

I have suggested that creativity in the primary classroom will involve the same elements of people, processes and domains and I have introduced the notion of creativity as an expression of holism. These latter two ideas will be discussed further in Chapter 8.

3 Creativity and play

In this chapter, I explore relationships between play and creativity. In doing so, I draw a distinction between fostering playful ideas and enabling bodily play and ask how far play can necessarily be described as creative. I turn next to practical implications for teaching and learning and finally I look at the formal curriculum for the early years and for older primary children and some of the issues which these raise for fostering children's creativity through play.

Play and creativity

Play and creativity in education are often conflated. A recent example of this can be found in the SCAA (1997) desirable learning outcomes for children's learning on entering compulsory education at age 5. These are grouped into six areas of learning which include 'creative development' as one. Creative development, in the SCAA formulation of it, focuses on 'the development of children's imagination and their ability to communicate and to express ideas and feelings in creative ways'. It includes the following:

> Children explore sound and colour, texture, shape, form and space in two and three dimensions. They respond in a variety of ways to what they see, hear, smell, touch and feel. Through art, music, dance, stories and imaginative play, they show an increasing ability to *use their imagination*, to listen and to observe. They use a widening range of materials, suitable tools, instruments and other resources to *express ideas and to communicate their feelings*.
>
> (SCAA, 1997: 85; my italics)

The SCAA formulation, then, appears to link play with creativity. The SCAA notion of 'creative development' places importance upon the imagination. It seems to me that in this document 'imagination' is being used to mean 'predicting', 'projecting' and 'considering possibilities' – aspects of everyday, or 'little c' creativity which I also emphasised in Chapter 1 of this book. As well as the imagination, emphasis is also placed by SCAA on communication; being 'in relationship' in these ways forms part of the model of creativity which I have proposed in Chapter 2.

The general creativity literature is also sprinkled with references to the importance of play in enabling creative thought, as indicated in Chapter 1. The notion of 'play' within the literature is wide, encompassing the creative process for both adults and children and incorporating playing around with ideas at one end and actual dramatic, bodily play at the other (this is similar to the spectrum proposed in Chapter 1 for creative outcomes, with ideas at one end and publicly acclaimed products at the other). On the play spectrum, creative cognitionists Ward, Finke and Smith (1995) suggest at the ideas end (and referring to learners of all ages):

> It is clear that we can abstract central properties, borrow analogies, merge concepts, change contexts and exploit preinventive forms to cultivate new ideas for sports, games, expressions, and personal products. Moreover, even if we never actually develop these ideas into realities, merely thinking about the creative possibilities can often be entertaining, rewarding, and enlightening.
>
> (Ward, Finke and Smith, 1995: 251)

At the other end, dramatic play theorists include Pepler (1982), cited in Chapter 1, suggesting that play which is structured so as to elicit non-standardised responses from children is more successful in fostering children's creativity in other tasks – and that social play together with adult intervention in stimulating imagination also helps. Dansky (1980) presents evidence that a strong element of fantasy in children's play is associated with more creativity in other contexts.

I want to take a closer look now at this spectrum of play as fostering ideas through to play as bodily activity.

Fostering playful ideas

Playful ideas, it seems to me, encompass a number of possible forms of thought. Supposing, imaging and being imaginative are three different processes involving the development and expression of playful ideas.

Supposing involves imagining or entertaining a hypothesis; it means thinking or acting 'as if'. It is a private process which may be shared and indeed developed by doing so. Imagining involves intention and may also include memory. I can intentionally imagine my first day in a new school, aged 6, when a bee stung me in the face during morning playtime – thus drawing on memory, with intention. Sometimes, however, the intention may be less conscious than in the first day at school example. A child at play can imagine what it might be like to be a pirate, or a doctor, or a princess. The process of becoming a princess or a pirate seems to be seamless with the child's real life, as I observe in my niece Natasha. One minute she is Natasha, aged 7, living in Kentish Town in London with her family, and the next she is Princess Natasha, who wears sparkly long dresses, high heeled shoes, lives in a palace and is going to marry a prince. Moments later she may be a ballerina, on a stage, and her living room is transformed into a theatre. Any adults or children in the room then become her captive audience whilst she dances for them. Moments later Natasha may re-emerge in her real-life self, to go swimming, or to get ready for dinner. And supposing may happen as ideas in Natasha's head, as well as being manifest in bodily play.

Supposing, then, may in certain contexts involve 'pretending' – indeed Ryle (1949) suggests that imagining is a species of pretending. This is so for children at play – and it is also the case for children and teachers, when learning their respective roles, that acting 'as if' they were teacher or pupil helps in taking on the mantle of that role.

Images, of which visual images are one sort, and of which olfactory, auditory, gustatory, etc. are others, involve a private process of some sort. Thus we say 'in the mind's eye' or 'having a song on the brain', whilst being at the time nowhere near genuine originals of the images produced. A child may recall their first school dinner, or the sound of their new-born sibling. Children's play, whether idea or bodily, often involves imaging. When Natasha is being a princess, she images her private ballroom, her flowing gowns with matching accessories and a range of sparkling jewels, even other princesses and princes to keep her company; she images comfy seats to rest on, beautiful gardens to play in and magical creatures who can make her wishes come true. Again, imaging is a part of both idea and bodily play.

Being imaginative involves, as indicated in Chapter 1, 'going beyond the obvious' or 'seeing more than is initially apparent' or interpreting something in a way which is unusual. Ten-year-old Jessica's description of mathematics as even boxes, is, it seems to me, being imaginative. Passmore (1980) has argued that being imaginative lies at the very heart of any free society.

Being imaginative, I have argued elsewhere (1988), must involve the agent being aware of the unconventionality of what they are doing/thinking. Thus, a child who invents a code to enable her to communicate with a sibling after lights out, is, it seems to me, being imaginative – whereas a child who becomes a character in their favourite TV programme, re-experiencing adventures which that character has had, is not necessarily being imaginative.

Being imaginative is distinct from fantasy. Several writers have pointed out that the fantasy can only recombine what is already known – in other words, that it involves non-imaginative imaging. If fantasy involves re-combinations of the known, it is close to 'fancy' as discussed by Kenny (1989) and to 'imaging'. In his account, Kenny uses the term 'fancy' to separate out imaging from being imaginative. For Kenny, the imagination, in contrast to the fancy, is creative, involving 'the ability to imagine the world different in significant ways; the ability to conjecture, hypothesise, invent . . . possessed *par excellence* by persons such as poets, story-tellers and scientists of genius' (p. 113). He suggests that imagination is superior to the intellect, as it enables the thinker 'to form new thoughts and discover new truths and build up new worlds' (p. 114). As he puts it, 'the objects of imagination are created, not discovered' (p. 117). The creative imagination is, according to Kenny, an aspect of the intellectual faculty. Thus he suggests the creative imagination seems to be both more disciplined and more original than the fancy. I have no difficulty with Kenny's distinction between fancy and imagination, nor with his account of either.

What is useful about Kenny's account is its attempt to flesh out the intellectual element of what we might call being imaginative, in contrast with the whimsical, 'supposition' based fancy, and with the free floatingness of fantasy. The lack of objective or direction in fantasy, the sense in which fantasy can involve ideas being 'blown' like a feather in the wind, is one of the reasons why I would distinguish it from being imaginative. Another is that dreams, hypnagogic states, nightmares, do not necessarily involve unconventionality or going beyond the given. Likewise, they do not necessarily involve intention to depart in some way from convention. Since imaginativeness necessarily involves the first two and depending on how intention is interpreted may involve the third, these states clearly do not qualify.

Fantasy, as Coleridge wrote 'has no other counters to play with, but fixities and definites' (cited by Jackson, 1969). In fact the interpretation of dreams relies upon this; taking into account that some of what is known is represented symbolically and therefore may be disguised in dreams. Being imaginative, by contrast, not only goes beyond the known as suggested earlier, but many writers, including Dewey, Montessori, Kant, de Bono (1967) and Barrow (1988) have claimed that being imaginative has an objective. As de Bono puts it: 'chaos by direction, not chaos through absence of direction' (p. 18).

It seems to me that these three major sets of processes, supposing, imaging and being imaginative, are all involved in play. The most significant in terms of being creative, however, is being imaginative or, as I shall sometimes call it, imaginativeness. It is this that I want to focus on next, looking at strategies for fostering it.

Strategies for fostering the capacity to be imaginative

Language is a critical element in fostering imaginativeness, whether in the context of bodily play or not. The philosopher of education Kenny (1989: 120) suggests that 'Everyone who uses language to make a supposition or frame a conjecture is using imagination.' This would include 'a parent inventing a bedtime story or a child playing consequences at a birthday party. The role playing of children typically involves both linguistic and non-linguistic elements, whether they are pretending to be jousting knights or doctors treating patients' (p. 120). Indeed, the SCAA desirable outcomes document referred to at the start of this chapter includes talk as an important element in fostering children's creative development, as follows, by emphasising the importance of assessment as a baseline in providing appropriate learning opportunities: 'it is not always possible to infer what a child can do from observations alone, or recorded work alone. Talking with children has a central role in assessing their understanding, and it is often through talk that a fuller picture of what a child can do is gained' (SCAA, 1997: 7).

Other writers emphasise structure, predictability and familiarity with both routines and the content of learning, which enables a learner to depart from what is known and to develop ideas which show imaginativeness. Lieberman (1977), for example, suggests that familiarity with setting and structure enable an individual to exercise imagination, to bend and twist the facts into different combinations. What Lieberman suggests is that playfulness operates at a point somewhere between familiar and novel aspects in the given facts and that the outcome of playfulness may be creative.

Warnock (1977) takes this a step further by suggesting that there is a connection between work and imagination, in that compulsion can offer a stimulus to seeing possibilities. She puts it thus:

> This is the connexion, then, between work and the imagination. For the imagination is the power to see possibilities, beyond the immediate; to perceive and feel the boundlessness of what is before one, the intricacies of a problem, the complications or subtleties of something previously scarcely noticed. To work at something, to begin to find it interesting, this is to begin to let the imagination play it ... So what school must offer is the chance to concentrate, whether on play or, equally, on work recognised as work, even if from time to time it seems uncongenial, merely a necessary task to be got through.
>
> (Warnock, 1977: 155)

She does, however, acknowledge the balance to be struck between compulsion in encouraging a child to enter the depths of a domain in order to foster playful ideas within it, and the need for learners to see the stimulus (and the compulsion) as relevant to them. The test of having succeeded in stimulating learners' imaginations, or not, is whether or not the school curriculum is perceived by the learner as boring. Schools should, Warnock suggests, provide stimulus to the imagination – through both 'work' and 'play'. She emphasises, however, that play itself needs stimulus – and can become boring if no longer relevant or interesting to the agent. She implies that playing can be even more boring than working if there is an element of choice and the choice is an unstimulating one. She emphasises that all which is done at school must be felt to have some point to it – whether intrinsic or extrinsic.

Passmore (1980) suggests that pedagogically there are a number of things which a teacher can do to foster imaginativeness:

1 '[they] can impart information in such a way as to suggest that there are genuine alternatives, in a manner which can set the imagination to work' (p. 162).
2 'He can teach routines ... as something which had to be imaginatively worked out; he can encourage the child to reflect on possible alternatives to them' (p. 162).

3   'the teacher can introduce the pupil to "possible worlds", opening up his mind to alternative modes of feeling, living' (pp. 162–163).

4   'Through the study of art he can help the child to see the world differently' (p. 163).

5   'In teaching mathematics and science, he can bring home to the child the importance of imaginative leaps, enlarge the child's sense of wonder, show him that the world cannot be taken for granted' (p. 153).

6   'the child can acquire – in and through learning a discipline . . . – the capacity to move beyond his everyday observations, his everyday experiences, his everyday inferences' (p. 163).

I want to emphasise that in developing strategies to support individual children's playful ideas there are no panaceas. Individuals need unique combinations of conditions. Five-year-old Rachel may need solitude, time and physical space above the companionship, discussion and physical proximity needed by 6-year-old Jacob. Ten-year-old Louis may need the information section of his local library, holidays in the Lake District and access to the Internet more than the tight friendship circles, horse-riding classes and girls' adventure stories drawn upon by 11-year-old Harriet. Age and gender may form a part of the set of influencing factors, but I would nevertheless want to emphasise the need to know each learner as an individual, to know what they may need at any point in time, to foster their own playful ideas.

Bodily play

I am terming 'bodily play' as distinct from playing with ideas, although of course there are overlaps in these terms, in that much bodily play may also involve playing with ideas of the kind discussed above, as the examples showed.

Much bodily play, as Cohen and MacKeith (1991) suggest, is ephemeral, involving being 'in the moment'. It may or may not involve insight, and children may slip virtually seamlessly from imitative play, which simply repeats what they have seen or experienced in another context, to highly imaginative activity, which involves supposing that their surroundings and companions represent something other than what they are. It is the imaginative end of this spectrum which I see as contributing to children's creativity.

Imaginative play at one extreme may lead children to develop 'paracosms' – long-term imaginary worlds (coined by Silvey and MacKeith; Cohen and MacKeith, 1991), which involve insight, long-term interest over months or years, pride and consistency, and a feeling in the child that their world matters to them. At the other it may involve dramatic play for just ten minutes whilst the 4-year-old goes to visit a monster on the moon in a hot air balloon with two friends, on the living room sofa, in a venture which is never repeated. At the paracosm end, Cohen and MacKeith suggest that children as young as 3 and as old as 13 may develop these.

There are many theories of bodily play – whether or not play leads to the outcome of a paracosm. These theories underpin and influence the sorts of practical bodily play opportunities which are offered to children. As Bruce (1991) notes, some theories imply that play is somehow an added extra, either for *discharging* energy (stemming from Schiller, summarised by Wilkinson and Willoughby, 1967) or for *recharging it* (stemming from Schaller (1861) and Lazarus (1883), who suggested that the role of play was to restore energy, to provide recuperation from work).

Other theories put play at the centre of education. Bruce (1991) characterises six different major theories which place play at the centre of learning.

1 Recapitulation theory: play reflecting culture – based on the work of Stanley Hall, 1884–1924.
2 Practice theory: play as preparation for adult life, based on the work of Groos, 1922 and Bruner, 1983. This theory of play often becomes adult dominated, turning into 'guided play', 'structured play', etc.
3 Cognitive development theories: play as the basis of learning rules, systems and knowledge. Based on the work of Piaget from the 1950s, 1960s and 1970s in particular (emphasising the role of practical experimentation of individual children in intellectual growth), Bruner from the 1960s onward (emphasising the social element in play in helping to introduce intellectual challenges which replicate adult life), and Vygotsky (emphasising the social elements of play as helping introduce the boundary of known and not yet known, and the potential for negotiating understanding with others including adults; this has been developed by more recent theorists such as Wood and Atfield, 1996).
4 Affective theories: based on many different authors, the main idea being that through play, children became 'integrated people'. Authors include Freud (seeing play as cathartic – enabling children to feel mastery and control), Erikson (an eight-stage developmental theory, emphasising children as partners in their own futures, working with metaphor in their play), Winnicott (a theory based around the significance of the transitional object).
5 Affective and cognitive: based around Millar's (1968) ideas that play enables the imitation of and experimentation with, social behaviour in a safe place.

Bruce has also developed her own theory of play: *free-flow play* (Bruce, 1991 and 1994). From a child-centred stance, she argues that play is a part of adult and child learning and living, proposing commonalities in free-flow play across cultures. She proposes that free play enables children to explore and become competent, as summarised in her equation (1991: 42):

Free-flow play = wallow + competence

She suggests that free-flow play has twelve features:

1   It is an active process without a product.
2   It is intrinsically motivated.
3   It exerts no external pressure to conform to rules, pressures, goals, tasks or definite direction.
4   It is about possible, alternative worlds, which involve 'supposing' . . . it involves being creative, imaginative, innovative.
5   It is about participants wallowing in ideas, feelings, relationships – and reflecting on and becoming aware of what is known.
6   It actively uses firsthand experiences (including struggle, manipulation, exploration, discovery, practice).
7   It is sustained, and when in full flow, helps us to function in advance of real-life scenarios.
8   We use previously developed technical prowess, mastery and competence during free-flow play, facilitating control.
9   Can be initiated by child or adult – but if the latter, s/he must pay particular attention to features 3, 5 and 11.
10 It can be solitary.
11 It can be in partnerships who will be sensitive to each other.
12 It is an integrating mechanism enabling us to bring together everything which we know, learn, feel, and understand.

Thus, for Bruce, free flow play means wallowing in ideas, feelings and relationships combined with application of developed competence, mastery and control.

Bruce suggests three major strategies for encouraging rich free-flow play:

1   Good observation and recording of children's play.
2   Supporting free-flow play through familiar context and through first hand experience.
3   Extending the child's experiences, using the familiar to introduce the unfamiliar.

She suggests that 'free flow playing respects individuals and encourages group sensitivity. It is about functioning . . . at a high level, and leads to quality in the way that the individuals interact with the sciences . . . and the arts' (1994: 190). She considers play to be an aspect of society's infrastructure. She also suggests that by neglecting it in the school system, problems are being stored up for the future.

It is important to recognise the variety of underpinning theories of play, since these affect how children are offered play opportunities, what is valued, the extent to which play is structured, how this may take place (i.e. direct or indirect), and by whom (by adult or by child).

Of course, each education practitioner is driven by a unique mix of theoretical and belief positions which underpins their practice in working with children generally and fostering their bodily play in particular. It seems to me that some theories of play encourage more creativity than others. For example, recapitulation theory and practice theory, it seems to me, both emphasise imitation, rather than innovation. They do not seem to be focused on fostering a child's creativity through play. On the other hand, free-flow play does seem to be concerned with enabling the child to innovate, to invent, to see through ideas in practice.

I would suggest, then, that the question of whether or not bodily play is conflatable with creativity within education rests heavily on the particular mix of theories and beliefs which drives each teacher or facilitator of children's learning. I return to the question of how far play is equivalent to creativity later in the chapter.

Play, gender and creativity

Gender plays an important role in play. As noted by Hargreaves and Hargreaves (1997), play is typically gendered in European and North American homes. Boys tend toward large, object-focused play. Girls tend toward quieter and more intellectual activities, which are more person-orientated. There may be implications for creativity – indeed Cohen and MacKeith (1991) cited earlier as researchers looking at children's paracosms, or long-term imaginary worlds, found that girls were more prone to develop people-focused paracosms than boys: 'far more than girls, boys tend to create these rather literal worlds . . . only about one in ten of the boys' worlds emphasised dramas between the various characters who peopled them. As fantasies go they tended to be rather impersonal' (p. 104). In contrast, girls 'produced more personal fantasies' . . . (p. 104). Whether there may be other implications of gendered play for creativity is, to my knowledge, yet to be discovered.

Summing up so far

In this chapter so far I have introduced the conflation of play and creativity, looking at both the SCAA desirable outcome of creative development and also some of the creativity literature. I have drawn a distinction between

- playful ideas, and
- bodily play.

Although distinct, there is overlap between these concepts.

In sketching out what playful ideas involve, I outlined a set of distinctions frequently used in philosophy of education:

- imagining,
- imaging, and
- being imaginative.

I have suggested ways in which each of these is involved in children's play. I proposed that being imaginative is most relevant in being creative and, drawing on the work of a range of writers, I suggested a range of pedagogic strategies for fostering the capacity to be imaginative:

- using language to both stimulate and assess imaginativeness;
- fostering familiarity with structure – and enabling children to participate in the creation of new routines where appropriate, reflecting on genuine possible alternatives;
- providing the environment in which children can go beyond what is offered (Warnock described this in terms of 'compulsion');
- helping children to find relevance in learning activities;
- modelling the existence of alternatives in the way information is imparted;
- encouraging children to consider alternative ways of being and doing;
- through art, helping children to view the world in a different way;
- through science and maths, helping children to understand how imaginative leaps are used to alter whole perceptions of the world;
- fostering the learning of any discipline in depth, to enable children's ability to go beyond their own immediate experiences and observations.

I suggested that there are no panaceas and that individual children may need different combinations of pedagogic strategies.

In looking at bodily play, I noted its often ephemeral nature but outlined a spectrum at one end of which is play which happens once and is not repeated, and at the other end of which is the creation of 'paracosms', or long-term imaginative worlds.

I outlined a number of theories of bodily play, noting that 'discharging' and 'recharging' are two which view play as an 'extra'. Theories which place play at the centre of learning, include:

- recapitulation theory;
- practice theory;
- cognitive development theories;

- affective theories;
- affective and cognitive theories.

I described Bruce's theory of free-flow play and its principles and suggested that some theories of play value the creative aspects of it more than others. Thus, the extent to which creativity can be meaningfully conflated with play in practice, rests in part on the unique mix of underpinning theories of play held by the educator.

Finally, I acknowledged briefly that play in western cultures appears to be quite gendered.

The next part of this chapter examines further the conflation of playfulness and creativity – and implications of this discussion for practice.

Playfulness and creativity

It has been argued (Lieberman, 1977) that there are links between playfulness in children and creativity in adults. Crudely put: the more you play as a child, the more creative you become in later life, in that playfulness ultimately becomes 'a personality trait of the individual and a possible clue to cognitive style' (p. 6). Lieberman suggests that 'playfulness is made up of spontaneity, manifest joy, and sense of humor' (p. 6). Based on empirical studies of kindergarten children and adult learners, plus their teachers, she concludes that 'the playful element is incorporated into experimentation' (p. 61).

She also suggests that where the teacher was playful, children were more creative: 'divergent thinking did occur in the pupils when the teachers were playful' (p. 59). She also concluded that playfulness becomes less acceptable as the individual grows up: 'Physical and cognitive spontaneity seem to fall by the wayside; manifest joy and sense of humor may be tolerated at times' (p. 55).

Is play necessarily creative?

Children spend an enormous amount of time playing and learning through idea and bodily play. To a degree, all idea and bodily play involves possibility thinking – which can be seen as the engine of playing with ideas. So far in this chapter I have looked at a variety of ways in which play is conflated with creativity and have introduced some examples of play in which behaviour may also be described as creative.

I would argue, however, that play is not necessarily creative. Imaginative play may border fantasy. A nursery child who over a long period of time role-plays being one of Batman's special helpers, or who continually dresses up as a princess, may be maintaining and developing a long-term role, but without being able to distinguish between fantasy and reality. I would not term this being creative, for creativity it seems to me must involve some insight into actions and ideas, as indicated in Chapter 1.

Play that is little more than imitation of other observed behaviours or scenarios is not creative, either, I would suggest. Yet, much of children's play has a high imitative content – and this has significance for development and socialisation. Much play, too, involves a combination of both imitation and fantasy – take Tom, who at the age of 6 insisted on being called Mortimore – the bird creature in a children's cartoon. He took on the role drawing on what he knew of the character from television, and fantasised new worlds, characteristics and experiences for Mortimore. For Tom, Mortimore offered an opportunity to model saying 'No' to those around him and a rich variety of ways in which to do the unexpected. But, although eccentric, I would not describe Tom's behaviour as creative since the main elements in it were imitation and fantasy. His behaviour was not driven by going beyond the obvious, in an independently-spirited way, and with insight.

By contrast, some play is highly creative – take for example the 'paracosms' or long-term imaginary worlds developed by some children, as researched and discussed by Cohen and MacKeith (1991).

The conflation, then, of play with creativity is, it seems to me, mistaken. However, play may provide certain important qualities for enabling children's creativity. What play and creativity have in common, I would suggest, is being driven by openness to 'possibilities'. Many writers, including Moyles (1994), have found that through play, children first explore, then use knowledge, then recognise and later solve problems using it. Later they practise and revise the knowledge and skill involved, for future use. Play therefore builds the child's confidence in being able to learn about their world. Making mistakes is an important part of this process: mistakes can be viewed as positive learning rather than errors never to be repeated.

Implications for practice

Although play is not the same process as creativity, there is some evidence that play may lead to greater creativity in children.

There is some evidence that children who have plenty of play experiences which invoke non-standardised responses (for example, engaging with non-structured and also multi-purpose play objects, and also getting involved in dramatic play) are more readily creative in other tasks (Pepler, 1982). So, play that has a strong imitative, intellectual, convergent or neutral 'flavour' seems to foster less creativity than experimental play, or what I call 'possibility playing'. It seems from some evidence that social play is more conducive to creativity than solitary play, and that adult intervention to stimulate imagination helps (Pepler, 1982). Dansky (1980) has demonstrated that children who are highly predisposed toward fantasy in their play are more likely to be imaginative in a task situation – also that some children are more predisposed toward fantasy play than others. Thus, although fantasy itself may be described, as I have done in the section above, as non-creative, a predisposition toward fantasy may ultimately contribute toward a child's creative abilities.

Garvey (1982) has suggested that play is linked with intellectual development. Being a good fantasiser seems to be linked with the development of imagination and intellectual skills as indicated earlier. According to Singer and Singer (1977), who investigated children who were good at fantasising, good fantasisers have better concentration, are less aggressive, and take more pleasure in what they do than children who fantasise less. Tower and Singer (1980) argued that children who were adept at imagining would develop better social and cognitive skills, integrating experiences better, learning the differences between what were inner and outer experiences, learning to organise information, being more reflective and developing superior concentration. They therefore recommended that parents join in fantasy games with children.

Some practical implications of research on play for teachers, include:

- providing opportunities for children to suppose, or to imagine;
- encouraging play which involves open-ended and non-standardised responses;
- offering opportunities and models for children to play both independently and together during the school day;
- allowing time for children to do all of the above and for teachers to support it;
- that possibility thinking is not just about what happens in classrooms; playtimes, assemblies, school visits and the playground, corridors and dinner halls all provide rich potential for supporting it;
- that some children will find it easier than others to engage with possibility thinking and possibility play; and
- that fantasy play may have a place underpinning cognitive development, particularly when supported in a deep fashion by parents, thus encouraging parental involvement may be helpful.

There are, of course, tensions between structure and freedom; the paradox in how to achieve an appropriate balance between the structuring of play and enabling the child complete freedom of choice in play is a contentious one. On the other hand, and more recently, Hargreaves and Hargreaves (1997) argue that it is not yet clear enough what kinds of play specifically lead to what kinds of cognitive outcomes.

Summing up – play and creativity

In this part of the chapter I have noted claims made by Lieberman about links between childhood play and creativity in later life, but have suggested that play of itself is not necessarily creative. Both fantasy and imitation form a significant part of much play and, I argued, neither is necessarily creative. On the other hand, some play is highly creative, for example the creation of paracosms. I suggested that what play and creativity have in common is the openness to possibilities.

I drew on a range of evidence which suggests that:

- exposure to play experiences which demand non-standardised responses is likely to foster more creativity in children across other tasks;
- social play is more conducive to creativity than solitary play;
- predisposition towards fantasy may contribute ultimately toward greater creativity.

I therefore proposed a range of practical strategies for supporting creativity, but also noted the inevitable tension between structure and freedom – and that it is not yet clear what kinds of play lead to what kinds of cognitive outcomes.

In the final part of the chapter I look at play in the curriculum.

Play in the curriculum

The National Curriculum

It has been argued by Anning (1994) that the National Curriculum is a partial one, in part because it gives almost no place to play within it. She suggests that it is underpinned by a values framework which belongs to a masculine, class-biased group, for whom play is a frivolous activity. She argues that since the early years profession has a weak record of researching rigorously, documenting and articulating professional thinking, the imposition of the National Curriculum model has been a powerful force which has altered the balance of what is valued and done in infant classrooms. It seems to me that this same analysis could be applied to the upper primary age range also, although clearly play in school has traditionally had a smaller role as children grow older.

Others, such as Wood and Atfield (1996) make a similar argument, noting that the 'New Right' which has generated the National Curriculum, diminishes play and its role in children's development. Embedded in some arguments criticising the introduction of a National Curriculum which gives little place to play is the feeling that it is too instrumental. For example, in a recent work Moyles (1997) argues that child-centred learning is the opposite of a curriculum which she believes is driven by economic and industrial concerns.

I would challenge Moyles's stance, however, and the view described above which considers play to be marginalised by the National Curriculum. For it is my view that a child-centred curriculum can also involve engagement with the world beyond schools and education as I have argued elsewhere (Craft, 1995).

Indeed it very often does; take, for instance, the topics of children's role play. Shops, travel, making of things, service industries such as cafes, etc. are just as common as complete fantasy scenarios such as monster caves and space flights to alien places.

As to the lack of emphasis on play in the National Curriculum, it seems to me that the potential for creative development does exist within some parts of the Key Stage 1 National Curriculum, particularly that of English, design and technology, information technology, art, music and PE. In different ways, these subjects encourage the representation of understanding and of feelings; also the skills of problem identification and problem solving: the asking and following through of 'what if?' questions.

Within the National Curriculum for older children, playing with ideas and bodily play are certainly far less explicit aspects of the content laid down in the subject orders. It seems to me, however, that playing with ideas is required to a significant degree in the curriculum for English, mathematics, science, design and technology, information technology, art and limited aspects of geography. Bodily play is required by aspects of the music curriculum and the physical education curriculum. In addition, it could be argued that the National Curriculum provides a content framework only, and, bar literacy and numeracy, not the pedagogical constraint – leaving teachers free to exercise their artistry in this respect.

SCAA's desirable learning outcomes: creative development

Creative development as one of the SCAA desirable learning outcomes, touched on at the start of this chapter, is perhaps more significant in terms of the role of play in creativity.

The fact that creative development is given a named place in the curriculum for children up until the age of 5, is important. As indicated earlier, it is one of the six areas of learning outcomes specified by SCAA. And creative development, in this representation of it, seems to involve fostering the ways in which children use their imaginations for representation and interpretation.

It is fairly domain-specific, in that imagination seems to encompass 'predicting', 'projecting' and 'considering possibilities' in the expressive and creative arts. The SCAA perspective reflects approaches developed by others (Edwards, 1990), which emphasise feelings and the creative arts. By contrast, and as argued by Feldman *et al.* (1994), I would argue that the notion of 'possibility' as fundamental to creativity, is not simply relevant in the arts but across *all* the domains of human endeavour. Indeed, I propose 'possibility thinking' as cross-curricular, as discussed in Chapter 1.

I have, nevertheless, argued elsewhere (Craft, 1999) that the inclusion of creative development in the early years curriculum is significant, from several points of view. First, it appears to validate child-centred play for the youngest children in education. It can be seen as an extension of previous early years provision which valued child-centred play (Bruce, 1991, 1994; Moyles, 1997; Wells, 1987). It seems to me that traditional parts of the early years curriculum can be seen as both contributing to and providing expression outlets for children's learning, meaning-making, interpretation, evaluation, at an intuitive, 'feelings' level – what Winnicott (1971) might perhaps view as 'unconscious'. It could be regarded as, in part, a counter-movement to what Bruce (1994: 197) calls the 'erosion of adults valuing children's free-flow play in complex industrial societies'.

Earlier in this chapter I outlined five dominant theories of play described by Bruce (1991) and a sixth one developed by Bruce (1991). It seems to me, as I have argued elsewhere (Craft, 1999) that SCAA's characterisation of creative development may reflect three of these, namely recapitulation theory (play as reflection of culture), practice theory (play as preparing for life as an adult) and cognitive development (play as learning rules, knowledge, systems).

Creative development may also be recognised as a break with the 'New Right' conceptions of curriculum embedded in the National Curriculum. For the SCAA creative development learning outcomes represent an endorsement of existing early years practice which values the potential of play to enable children's self-actualisation. In this sense it runs counter to the trend of marginalising play and the encroachment into the curriculum of the 'language of the marketplace' (Wood and Atfield, 1996: 14).

Another significant aspect of creative development, as I have argued elsewhere (Craft, 1999), is that it may be seen as promoting three particular conceptions of creativity. First, a humanistic conception of creativity, as a form of what Maslow called 'self-actualisation' (1971), meaning self-direction in the world at a variety of levels. It also implies a psychosynthetic perspective, drawing on the ideas of Assagioli (1974) and Fritz (1943), which sees creativity as involving conscious choice over levels of unconscious processes. And, third, it seems to me to imply a creative cognition perspective (which emphasises the generation and exploration of ideas using cognitive strategies including metaphor, analogies, mental models, schemas, visualising and the invention of new concepts) as described by Ward, Finke and Smith (1995). These are three perspectives on the phenomenon of creativity, from a much wider range of theoretical perspectives which include Freudian, information processing and Skinnerian.

Creative development appears to involve the whole brain (the left emphasising logic, language, mathematical representations, sequencing, linearity, and the right spatial manipulations, form and pattern, the imagination, rhythm and musical appreciation, intuition, images), as described by Brierley (1987) and Zdenek (1985). As such it may be seen as representing a holistic approach to learning.

Curriculum discontinuity

Clearly, the existence of the SCAA early years curriculum, alongside the National Curriculum, does present a curriculum discontinuity. For children over the age of 5 are subject to the National Curriculum, which does not include creative development within its parameters, although the potential for creative development does exist within some parts of the Key Stage 1 National Curriculum as discussed earlier. Thus aspects of the Key Stage 1 curriculum can be seen as providing some extensions of the early years curriculum for creative development (Craft, 1999). A glaring omission, however, once children turn 5, is the many aspects of play which are officially endorsed as the desirable outcome of creative development in the early years curriculum. This inevitably poses a range of challenges for educators, as follows. -

Assessment

Planning new learning from existing understanding and the child's current perspective/s on the domain which they are exploring, necessarily stems from effective assessment. In the case of creative development, as in the case of other domains, this means developing a close familiarity with each child's engagement in the aspects of creative development. The process of doing so may demand involvement and interaction in a variety of ways, as children invite conversation with or participation from the adults around them, particularly in bodily play. Indeed Bruce (1991) suggests a range of strategies to encourage rich free-flow play. Amongst these are observation and recording.

Observation of 3–6 year olds often intertwines with intervention, as assessment feeds in to planning and learning. This is so whether we are observing and working with individuals, or children working together.

The observation, recording and reporting of creative behaviour poses particular problems, similar to those identified by Wood and Atfield (1996) in exploring assessment issues in play. These include the need to ensure observation of children alone, together and with adults; and a sensitivity to the patterns and sources of children's self-initiated activities.

Discontinuity in values

Much of my discussion so far has drawn on the notion of creative development as defined and expressed in the laid down curriculum. But another of the challenges is the value and importance which teachers and policy makers themselves place on creative development.

There are at least two aspects to this. One: the discontinuity in the curriculum between the early years desirable outcomes and the National Curriculum means that educators must question how best to support children across the transition between one curriculum and another (Hurst, 1997). One aspect of the puzzle is what to do about play – both the process and the content. How far should the children be encouraged to explore the ten National Curriculum subjects through play? What will happen to some of the physical resources for play which now appear more marginalised in the curriculum – the home corner, the shop, the doctors' surgery, not to mention large and small blocks, also figures, puppets, etc.?

Two: the dual curriculum raises the age-old question of how to manage teaching time. Evidence from the infant classroom suggests a domination of seat-based tasks involving literacy and numeracy. An aspect of this is the separation of 'real learning' (sometimes known as 'curriculum 1' and involving the cognitive basics of literacy and numeracy) from 'play' or 'choosing' (sometimes known as 'curriculum 2' and involving practical activities including painting, drawing, role play, etc.). This division often corresponds to the parts of the day which are perceived to offer different levels of value in terms of children's concentration – mornings often being when the real work is done, and afternoons when childen are allowed to choose.

Organisation and resourcing

The organisation and resourcing of the physical learning environment, in combination with the roles adults adopt within it, need to be carefully considered in the light of how they contribute to children's creative development. Modelling, or even 'mentoring', creative play behaviour forms a part of this.

Creative development as arts based

As noted earlier, creative development is defined by SCAA and the DfEE as involving the creative and expressive arts only. This approach perpetuates the myth that creativity is just to do with the arts. It seems to me that creative development has the potential to support learning, exploration and expression right across the curriculum, not just in the creative and expressive arts.

Summing up – play, the curriculum and creativity

In this final part of the chapter I have noted concerns, expressed by several writers and researchers in the field of play, that the National Curriculum marginalises children's play in an unhelpful way. I challenged this perspective, suggesting:

- the National Curriculum whilst relating children's learning to life beyond school and beyond childhood, also offers scope for play, in a variety of ways;
- children themselves often bring the world beyond school into their learning; and
- whilst specifying content, the National Curriculum itself does not specify pedagogy – except in the literacy and numeracy strategies.

Of greater concern, I suggested, are the discontinuities between the

National Curriculum and the SCAA desirable learning outcomes, particularly for children in the first year of school where both curricula are in operation. I suggested:

- the early years curriculum itself is problematic in that it implies that creative development is linked closely with the arts; an assumption I would challenge;
- on the other hand, the inclusion of play within that curriculum does represent continuity with previous 'best practice' in early years provision;
- that the inclusion of creative development in the early years curriculum seems to represent humanistic, psychosynthetic and creative cognition approaches to creativity itself, and that it appears to be a holistic approach in the sense of involving both left and right hemispheres of the brain;
- that discontinuities and areas of concern, however, include assessment, discontinuities in values, organisation and resourcing and creative development as arts based.

The development of children's creativity is an important part of what educators and learning systems do. The identification of creative development in the early years curriculum makes an attempt to acknowledge important aspects of creativity, but the restriction of these to only certain parts of human existence and expression, combined with the serious discontinuity between the early years and the National Curriculum, means that educators are faced with considerable practical challenges in achieving this.

Claxton (1984: 228) has said, 'To be creative you have to dare to be different.' What is clear is that the development of creativity skills, through daring to be different, must go on at the dual levels of both policy and practice.

Part II

Creativity across the curriculum

4   The arts and humanities

In this chapter I look first at how the arts have traditionally been seen as embodying and supporting creativity as reflections of and tools for analysing, aspects of life. Starting with the sensory overlaps with science, I explore creativity in the performing, visual and expressive arts in school as enabling children to do, analyse and feel. I go on to examine ways in which learning in the humanities demands creativity of both children and teachers.

Arts and sciences – a polarity in reality?

The arts and humanities are often contrasted in a polarity with science, maths and information technology. Some have even argued that the coming of the National Curriculum has so altered the balance of science in primary education that the curriculum is 'led' by science in many schools (Taylor and Andrews, 1993). They suggest

> in many schools, a whole year's projects and topics are definitively listed in advance on staffroom notice boards, ensuring an inflexibility in learning – inert and sterile . . . with cursory, superficial approaches to topic work, the arts frequently featuring as little more than servicing agencies for a science-driven curriculum.
>
> (Taylor and Andrews, 1993: 131–132)

It seems to me that embedded in some criticisms of the science-led curriculum is the belief that one of the differences between the arts/humanities and sciences is in the extent to which each subject involves or encourages creativity. I call this the 'polarity perspective'. Contrary to this 'polarity perspective', I believe that each subject demands and fosters creativity. Consequently, I explore in Chapters 5 and 6 how creativity is involved in the learning and teaching of maths, science, IT and design and technology.

It seems to me that there is a common dimension in the creativity of the sciences and arts/humanities: the sensory aspect. Sensory experience is particularly relevant to science. It can be seen as forming a bridge, or even a place of overlap between the arts and science (as argued by Best, 1990 and Taylor and Andrews, 1993).

I would argue that the different purposes played by sensory experiences in the arts and in the sciences should be explicitly drawn out with the children. Thus, handling different kinds of materials may form part of a science activity. In contrast, observing them closely looking at line, texture, colour, imagining their history or future through play and fantasy may form part of an arts activity. Watching the stick insects or looking after the class hamster may form part of the science curriculum in explaining behaviour, growth, habitat and camouflage, feeding and reproduction. Handling, smelling, listening to and observing them may provide stimulus for creating, for example, poems, paintings, models, role play, dance.

The purposes you intend will dictate, then, the way in which you set up sensory learning experiences. I would argue, with Taylor and Andrews, that domination of the curriculum by science-led activities is not necessary, and that the polarity of creativity, with the arts at one end and science at the other, is perceived and not real.

The creative arts and education for being

A concept I find useful in the context of creativity in the arts and humanities is 'education for being' (Fontana, 1994, 1997). By this Fontana means offering children

> the right to express their own feelings, to give their view of events, to explain themselves, to reflect upon their own behaviour, to have their fears and their hopes taken seriously, to ask questions, to seek explanations in the natural world, to love and be loved, to have their inner world of dreams and fantasies and imaginings taken seriously, and to make their own engagement with life.
>
> (Fontana, 1997: 13)

An education for being is about 'quality rather than quantity' (p. 14). It is about fully appreciating and becoming bound up in the totality of the global environment, including the people in it. It is, as Fontana puts it,

> an education that teaches children to understand and respect themselves, to empathise with others, to show a care and a concern for the world in which we live, to remain sensitive to the inner world of dreams, reflections and imaginings, to remain in awe of the wonders of creation, to give and receive love and understand the meaning of loving relationships, to express feelings and accept such expression in others, to identify worthwhile life goals and means towards their attainment, and to develop and articulate a mature philosophy of life that makes sense of the world and one's own place within it.
>
> (Fontana, 1997: 14)

During the 1980s, Maslow developed the concept of 'self-actualisation' – in other words, adults who seem able to have become whole and complete people (1987). He noted that such people shared the following characteristics:

- being emotionally open;
- spontaneity and 'being natural';
- being problem focused rather than self-focused;
- being content with their own company;
- having personal autonomy in attitude;
- being accepting of self and others;
- being appreciative of life;
- capable of loving relationships;
- being humorous;
- being creative;
- having an ethical framework;
- operating to a democratic framework;
- being consistent.

The notion is of a self-actualised person as a psychologically healthy one. David Fontana argues, and I would support his perspective, that an education for being supports children in their self-actualisation.

The creative arts, then, offer ways of both developing forms of self-expression, and ways of exploring one's creativity (Fontana, 1997; Gardner, 1994; Walters *et al.*, 1996), through education for being. Another way of describing these two roles of the arts (expression and exploration) is that they offer ways of *making* and ways of *appraising* (Robinson *et al.*, 1990a, 1990b).

Theatre and possibility

The following is an excerpt from a talk given during 1996 by Christine Kimberley, formerly a Director of the Institute for Creativity. She spoke about the role of the Arts in fostering creativity.

> When we come into this world we have two gifts. The physical resources of the planet we live on, including of course our own bodies and imagination. Two gifts, apples and dreams. No matter where we are born, irrespective of culture, race, religion, political context, economic circumstances. Two gifts. And these two gifts are essentially neutral. Innocent. Free from moral wrong. With them we create to live.
>
> Imagination is the vehicle for change. First, we must imagine something is possible, then we can create a way of doing it.
>
> Unfortunately, sometimes we have a tendency to invest the neutral facility, the innocent ability to imagine with the burden of outcome. It becomes tangled with the responsibility for moral wrong – and often with guilt, failure and even punishment.

It is then that we keep our imaginings to ourselves and feel powerless in the face of change – in the face of other people's imaginings.

There is a place where our imagination can run free. Where we can experiment and explore. Explore the 'what if' – safely free from the burden of outcome. This place for me is live Theatre. I believe it is true of the other arts too, but Theatre is my speciality.

In Theatre, Imagination is practised, honoured, respected, experienced and witnessed, in innocence. For this very fact alone, Theatre is not a luxury or a pastime. It is an essential part of any robust, healthy society.

Theatre, like all the Arts, constantly reminds us that we have imagination. That imagination has infinite power to create possibility, diversity, solutions. In Theatre, we can explore death without dying. And without shedding a single drop of blood, we can reflect, judge, consider, discern and contemplate the most colossal or the most intimate of human dilemmas – in innocence.

I believe this is vital to us all. Particularly for young people, to have access to art and theatre – not just as doers, in taught classes, but as watchers, as audience.

In this capacity they have the chance to explore and to develop their own morals, ethics and so on through the act of witnessing. And, they are exposed to the impossible being made possible – as they are taken on an emotional, sensate journey – shown a story that they know to be both real and unreal all at once. Imagination in practice as they practice using their own. And this is the point, Theatre can't but encourage young people to wonder, to question, to use their imaginations, to explore possibilities. This is true learning as they learn to create their future.

(Kimberley, 1996)

The role within a society of the arts in general and of theatre in particular, is culturally and era-specific. What they provide within any one society may be described along a continuum with at one end 'challenging society' and in the middle of it 'reflecting society' (at the far end might be 'supporting society', or hegemony). Focusing on these two contrasting roles of challenge and reflection, Robinson *et al.* (1990b: 29) write,

> in some societies and at some times the artist is an iconoclast who challenges prevailing attitudes and values, generating new perceptions to challenge established ways of thinking. At others, artists are the 'voice of the community', shaping images and artefacts to give form to a community's deepest values and convictions.

The excerpt given above from Christine Kimberley's talk emphasises the role of theatre in allowing us to explore all kinds of possibilities. She talked of our having two resources: the physical environment of our planet, and our imaginations. How often do we as teachers utilise drama or theatre to enable children to draw on these two resources?

Creating, communicating and interpreting: the performing arts

Drama, music, dance, physical agility, poetry reading and storytelling are some of the most common forms of performance in schools. Each gives children opportunities to communicate, to interpret, and to create for themselves. Tambling (1990: 95) has argued, 'the arts are primarily about creativity and imagination'. It is important that we don't forget to encourage children to create for themselves, whether through story, rhythm, melody or choreography. Consider Morwenna.

Morwenna teaches Y5 children in a northern city, in a school committed to teaching the whole curriculum through an arts focus. She herself is musical, and performs on a regular basis in local pubs as a folk singer playing her guitar. She encourages the children to create their own drama, music, stories and dance as much as possible. At the end of each half-term of learning, she asks the children to work collaboratively in small groups to create a performance piece which for them summarises what they feel they have learned. After a recent project on local history, one group of five children composed a song accompanied by xylophone, drum, triangle and recorder, which outlined all that they had both enjoyed and learned in the project.

How often do the children you teach have such opportunities to interpret, create and communicate?

Where children are performing a piece created by someone else, there is an important dynamic between 'author' (the choreographer, writer, composer) and the performers – even where the children don't get the chance to meet the author. 'Being in relationship' is an important aspect of creativity. You can offer children ways of exploring what they consider the author's intentions to have been, and encourage exploration of possibilities in representing the work. Predicting how the author might then perceive the children's interpretations is a further aspect of fostering the children's creativity. Occasionally, it might even be possible to check out the author's intentions and reactions, face to face.

Creativity, or possibility approaches, can be fostered both *in* and *through* the arts: a notion explored by Robinson *et al.* (1990b), and which I will return to later when exploring the humanities.

Language, literacy and possibility

Language is a medium through which possibility can be explored. Like the performing arts, the creator (speaker or writer) can represent, analyse and express feelings. But what is different in the case of language is that particularly in the primary school, 'teaching the basics' is part of the focus. It has been argued (Taylor and Andrews, 1993) that the National Curriculum's definition of the language curriculum for schools has virtually divorced the learning of basic skills from the creative possibilities offered by language. I do not subscribe to this view. In contrast I would argue that even with very young children it is possible to encourage experimentation, analysis and the expression of feelings – and that the National Curriculum leaves plenty of room for so doing.

Consider story time in the reception class: sharing books together offers opportunities for analysis – for example, exploring characterisation, plot, presentation, illustration, the author's intentions. It is also an opportunity for exploring how the children feel about the story, as well as feelings within it. And there are plenty of ways in which story time can stimulate the children's own invention: predicting the ending, or thinking of alternative ones once you know how the story goes; making up rhymes and raps; inventing new characters; getting into character and exploring the relationships between characters in the story through drama . . .

Similarly, teaching writing skills in Y1 can offer many opportunities for children to create, alongside developing the basics. Handwriting practice can provide the basis for imaginative work, using, for example, poems and rhymes introduced and created verbally with the children during story times. The children's own writing at this age is often linked with their drawings: drawing their 'news' or 'writing about a picture' are common approaches. Although both involve the children making something, neither of these, however, is particularly creative. Other, more creative, possibilities include:

- conjecturing/exploring how something 'works' (such as the rising of dough, the growing of cress, or collage work done by a partner);
- responding to firsthand experiences (such as a walk in the park, a visit to a puppet theatre, holding the class hamster, watching the tadpoles grow);
- making signs for class-wide dramatic play (for example, turning the home corner into a hospital, a vet's or a shop);
- inventing characters (creatures or people), objects and events around which to design a story (this can be done individually, in pairs, groups or even as a whole-class activity);
- inventing five-word poems which embody their feelings about a particular event (such as bonfire night, a religious festival, an assembly by an older group of children or by themselves, a book they have read or had read to them, the birth of a sibling, the death of a pet).

Writing creatively may also be linked to other activities which themselves have potential for developing creativity, such as role play or reading. As the National Curriculum Council Oracy Project argued during the 1980s, oral language forms a vital part in fostering inspired written work in the classroom. With young children this is particularly so, as Cowie (1989) has documented; 3-year-olds are capable of composing stories using emergent writing and drawing, and can tell these aloud. We know from work by Scarlett and Wolf (1979), who explored ways in which children's imaginative writing was enhanced by props (e.g. a dragon, a castle, a royal family, little trees and toy animals), that 4-year-olds and upward are much more able to express their stories linguistically. The younger children needed much greater physical contact with their props in order to invent. From my own observations of under-4s, I would argue that encouraging and engaging in imaginative play with the children is vital to creativity. It can provide models of creating processes, and can stimulate the children's writing, particularly storying (i.e. the development of stories through a variety of means, often collaborative, and given a variety of forms of expression).

It seems to me, then, that opportunities for developing creativity do exist, even at the most basic levels of language and literacy. As the child's skill progresses, the opportunities extend, as their more skilful use of language enables them to both explore other people's compositions and create those of their own. Take this poem, written by Franny, aged 8.

> On a dark dark night
> When the dragon flies
> its breath as a tornado.
> Its roar as a big red blur.
>
> So do not come near
> Dragons here.
> He flies through
> the night and gives people a fright.
>
> Flap goes his wings
> As he hunts for his treasure,
> his wings go snap!, snap!, snap!.
> He swoops woooooooooooosh
>
> He hunts for prey
> So if you
> See him, run away.
> RUN AWAY!.

In her poem, Franny demonstrates a familiarity with mythical phraseology met in her reading (e.g. 'on a dark dark night'), onomatopoeia ('roar', 'flap', 'snap', 'woooooooosh') and similes ('its breath as a tornado', 'Its roar as a big blur'). She also demonstrates a growing, although as yet inaccurate, grasp of how and when to use exclamation marks ('RUN AWAY!.').

A 10-year-old girl I know has recently written a short story, which she loaned to me. With her permission, I reproduce the opening part of her story here:

> Mollana was clinging to his unicorn's mane, he was deafened by the pounding of her hooves on the white puffy clouds. Most people would think that if you stood on a cloud you would fall right through it, but you are wrong. Mollana could see the moon in the distance, a round, dappled, grey thing quivering and looking very shy. Mollana tried to slow his unicorn down to a trot. The unicorn was a grey, her mane was very long, longer than her glistening neck, her fringe went all the way down to her nose and when

it grew it grew in soft silky billowy waves, it was as if it was flowing silently down into a valley. She was called Dobbin.

They had reached the moon and could feel the soft scent of the sweet fresh air. One side of the moon had been completely destroyed by Mollana's enemy, Unmada. Unmada was a human, he often visited the moon in his rocket. He had dark brown greasy hair which was always gelled back. Mollana and Unmada had had a really diabolical fight and he had lost.

It all started when Mollana had come into the city and destroyed Unmada's house. He pulled all of the wallpaper off the walls, smashed all of the well polished windows, and screwed up all of the apple green carpets. Unmada had caused an inferno on Mollana's beloved moon. It had been a disastrous fight. Often Mollana would think back on the fight. He would cry even though he didn't know it, a small tear would trickle down his face missing his eye by a millimetre then carrying on till it floated silently off his face. Each tear of his that dropped on the ground would make a bit of Mollana's braveness and wisdom go, go forever and never come back.

(An extract from 'Mollana and Dobbin', by Harriet Quigley)

What leaps out of Harriet's writing for me is her capability in expressing what Wilkinson *et al.* (1980) term 'affect' (i.e. 'emotional, imaginative and inter-personal awareness'). This is demonstrated in 10-year-old Annie's poem too – this time inspired by E.V. Rieu's 'The Paint Box'.

The Paint Box

Paint me something utterly new,
Of course I won't tolerate that browny blue,
'I shall paint you anything you want at all,
How about a princess at a ball?'

That sounds great, fantastic, wow!
Can you paint her on me this minute now?
'I shall paint her on you with a sparkly shine,
If I can find that pallet of mine.'

Mix me a colour that really shows,
Paint her in a palace where nobody knows,
'I shall paint her better than that lovely tree,
You will never find a better artist than me'.

Evidence from Wilkinson *et al.*'s Crediton Project, which explored the writing of 150 children aged 7, 11 and 13, suggested that the younger children in the sample were less capable of expressing 'affect' than the older children.

Other work, by contrast (Graves, 1983), suggests that given the opportunities to draft, to discuss sources, to explore meaning and depth in their writing, young children are able to create imaginative, complex pieces. A number of researchers

(Graves, 1983; Cowie and Hanrott, 1984) argue that the following strategies help younger children's linguistic expression, including their writing. They are all aspects of developing what Graves named the 'writing community', and what I call a community of creators:

- encouraging children to work collaboratively for some of the time;
- allowing children control over their writing processes, which includes giving them time to compose;
- use of the word-processor by children for drafting, editing and re-drafting;
- emphasising a range of audiences for writing (such as for each other, for younger children, for oneself, for parents, for the local community, as well as for the teacher);
- entering into the children's imaginative worlds (which, as I noted in Chapter 3, can be immensely complex and also long-lasting, sometimes spanning years – Cohen and MacKeith, 1991);
- listening carefully to the children's views of and reactions to writing.

The arts and children's feelings

So far I have talked mainly about the performing, expressive and, to a limited extent, the visual arts as enabling both making and perceiving, in other words:

- fostering children's capabilities in doing or making; and
- enabling their abilities to perceive, analyse or explore what they are representing.

The arts play a further, important role in education, which is highlighted by Taylor and Andrews (1993) and also by Gardner (1994), and which should have become apparent in the poems above:

- enabling the exploration and expression of children's feelings.

A useful theory of rationality and feeling, put forward by Best (1992), is that children need to be introduced to the conventions and values of any particular art form in order to fully experience the 'relevant' feelings. Best's arguments are, of course, open to the charge of elitism and exclusivity.

However, there are two points embedded in his perspective which I would argue are valuable in the primary classroom. First, that the domains of existing knowledge and achievement are an important and, I would argue, necessary backdrop to exploring a 'feelings response' to art created by the children themselves and by others. Second, that children's feelings responses are probably deepened and broadened by an understanding of artistic genre and context. Meet, for example, Clare, developing the visual arts.

Clare taught Y5 children in a city primary school. She decided to devote a half term of art lessons to exploring expressionist painting techniques and the context to the expressionist movement. The children learned about some of the key expressionist painters and their lives by visiting several art galleries in London. Clare borrowed a selection of resources, including a number of reproduction paintings by expressionists, from the resource bank of her local education authority. The children's own art work included trying out various paint techniques, also painting replicas of particular reproductions in order to try these out.

The children's capability in exploring mood, movement, activity, relationships and so on as represented in famous artists' work was gradually enhanced over the six weeks of this unit of work.

I would argue that this tiny snapshot of Clare's practice represents the importance and the potential of exploring the domain to which any form of expression belongs, and the culture surrounding that domain. It also illustrates the role played by primary and secondary sources which formed part of the children's learning. The children's own creativity was encouraged within a defined context. Although this example is taken from visual art, the expression, experiencing and exploration of feelings is also a part of the performing and expressive arts.

Consider your own practice in, for example, drama, dance or writing. How could you develop your own strategies for immersing children in existing knowledge and achievement, whilst also giving them an opportunity to explore their feelings?

Risk and ownership

One of the biggest challenges for children when creating in the arts is having a go at making something which they can feel is their own. This can carry considerable risk for children, as they may create something which does not meet with the approval of the intended audience.

In addition, observers have noted (Hargreaves, Galton and Robinson, 1989) that primary teachers in particular often try to support children's creativity in the arts in a two-stage process (i.e. modelling, or giving a lot of guidance to begin with, followed by letting children have a go for themselves). However, the evidence suggests that this does not in fact foster children's creativity (Galton, 1987).

Instead, it seems (Armstrong, 1980; Rowlands, 1984) that what is really critical is that children understand the purposes of each activity, and the expectations of the teacher of what they are going to be doing. There is also a need to allow children time to incubate their ideas, and to come to terms with the challenges of risking failure, before 'owning' their creative work.

The arts and the National Curriculum

Significantly, the formulation of the National Curriculum gives the performing arts a rather minor place in the curriculum, subsuming these within English and physical education (PE). Also under-emphasised is the role of the arts in enabling children to explore and express feelings, and the element of risk involved in creating/presenting, for the process of being creative in the arts is presented as unproblematic and unemotional.

The National Curriculum for English in Key Stages 1 and 2 specifies that children should be offered opportunities for both evaluating the spoken, written and dramatic/improvised outcomes of others (children included) and creating their own outcomes. Thus it involves both making and ways of appraising (Robinson *et al.*, 1990a, 1990b), as discussed above. The fostering of imagination is emphasised in writing and reading in particular. The speaking and listening part of the English curriculum seems to emphasise critical and analytical thinking over creative thinking.

By contrast the subject orders for PE in Key Stages 1 and 2 specify dance as an area of activity, and emphasise the exploration of 'moods and feelings' in Key Stage 1 (DFE, 1995g: 3) and of 'moods, feelings and ideas' in Key Stage 2 (DFE, 1995g: 4). In both key stages responding to music and using this as a stimulus to create is also a requirement. As in English, the elements of risk involved in creating seem to me to be understated in the National Curriculum for dance within PE. And although the potential for reflecting culture, discussed above, is embedded in the subject orders (for example in Key Stage 2, pupils are to 'be taught . . . a number of dance forms from different times and places, including some traditional dances of the British Isles' – DFE, 1995g: 4), the potential for challenging culture through dance is not developed at all.

The National Curriculum for art in both Key Stage 1 and Key Stage 2 emphasises the importance of three elements: expressing, observing and making. The art curriculum is broad enough to incorporate craft and design as well as art. Affect (feelings), possibility and risk are key aspects of the National Curriculum for art, reflecting ideas discussed in this chapter. However, although art is seen as situated within culture in time and space, its potential for challenging shared beliefs is not drawn out.

The acknowledgement of cultural traditions is also embedded in the National Curriculum for music, however as with art and dance, the potential for music to challenge society is not. The music curriculum does, on the other hand, offer children the opportunity to 'compose in response to a variety of stimuli . . . communicate musical ideas to others' . . . and 'listen to, and develop understanding of, music from different times and places . . . respond to, and evaluate, live performances and recorded music, including their own and others' compositions and performances' – thus the triad of making, expressing, observing are all valued.

Summing up: the arts and creativity

I have explored ways in which the arts enable:

- the development of children's imaginations in making or doing;

- children's skills in analysing and interpreting;
- exploration and expression of the children's feelings.

I have explored the roles played by the arts in both reflecting and challenging society, at different times in different cultures. The arts enable communication. I have argued that introducing children to existing domains of artistic expression is an important part of developing their own creativity and appreciation of the creativity of others. I have suggested that fostering creativity in the arts can involve risk for the children and consequently needs incubation time.

Finally, I have offered a rough mapping of some of the ideas explored above on to the National Curriculum for English, PE, art and music. In doing so I have suggested that some aspects of the potential of the arts have been underdeveloped in the current version of the National Curriculum (1995), namely risk taking in creativity, expression and exploration of feelings and the potential of the arts to challenge culturally held assumptions and beliefs. All of these I consider important in the development of creativity in the arts and thus an omission in the 1995 National Curriculum.

Learning about, for and through the humanities

During the 1970s, Blyth and colleagues coined a way of thinking of the humanities as playing three roles in the 8–13 school curriculum, in that it was possible to educate *about, for and through* them (Blyth *et al.*, 1976).

These models are, in my view, still valid today, at the end of the 1990s, and are, I would suggest, just as relevant for much younger children. Learning about, through and for can be seen as three different and co-existent models of the curriculum. Learning *about* the humanities can be interpreted as a model of the curriculum as cultural transmission. Learning *for* the humanities implies a use of the knowledge and skills which will follow from the learning, and hence implies an instrumental or utilitarian view of curriculum. Learning *through* the humanities implies a developmental view of the curriculum where the personal 'sense-making' learning of individual children is more deeply emphasised than the transmission of a body of knowledge or the use to which this may be put later (Ahier and Ross, 1995).

Of course, the National Curriculum does provide a framework for learning *about*. In history, for example, the areas of study for Key Stage 1 are specified thus, 'pupils should be taught about the everyday life, work, leisure and culture of men, women and children in the past . . . about the lives of different kinds of famous men and women . . . about past events of different types' (DFE, 1995c: 2). The six study units for Key Stage 2 are also specified, including Romans, Anglo-Saxons and Vikings, Tudor times, Victorian Britain, life since 1930 in Britain, Ancient

Greece, local history and a past non-European society. The National Curriculum for geography specifies that pupils must be taught about specific things: in Key Stage 1, pupils are to be taught a range of information about places, and also about the quality of the environment as a thematic study. As an example of the knowledge specified, for places, the curriculum states that

pupils should be taught:
a) about the main physical and human features . . . that give localities their character;
b) how localities may be similar and how they may differ . . . ;
c) about the effects of weather on people and their surroundings . . . ;
d) how land and buildings . . . are used.

(DFE, 1995c: 3)

In Key Stage 2, pupils are to be taught a range of information about places, and also about the four geographical themes of rivers, weather, settlement and environmental change. An example of the information pupils are to learn about places is as follows:

pupils should be taught:
a) about the main physical and human features . . . that give localities their character;
b) how localities may be similar and how they may differ . . . ;
c) how the features of the localities influence the nature and location of human activities within them . . . ;
d) about recent or proposed changes in the localities . . . ;
e) how the localities are set within a broader geographical context.

(DFE, 1995c: 5)

To a lesser extent the National Curriculum also provides a framework for learning *for*. In history, the skills (or 'key elements', such as interpretations of history, historical enquiry and organisation and communication) which children are to develop in each study unit or area of study provide a foundation for applying historical enquiry and interpretation across other contexts and content. In geography, a range of cultural/social values are expressed through the selection of knowledge in the curriculum. For example, the Key Stage 1 thematic study is on the environment, implying a high value placed on citizenship in a community where interconnections are cherished. This aspect of geography, sometimes called 'social geography', is also apparent in Key Stage 2, where human impact on the landscape and economy is a part of the curriculum (under the theme of 'settlement') and the impact of people on their surroundings, both local and global, is a part of the theme 'environmental change'. The inclusion of these particularly social values implies that the curriculum is designed to educate *for* as well as *about*.

As to Blyth's concept of learning *through* history and geography, this is left much more down to the teacher.

Imagining different possibilities

Just as theatre enables us to explore imaginative possibilities in life, so history and geography can provide ways in to understanding multiple perspectives on aspects of life. It seems to me that the humanities in particular offer children a model of imagination and creativity, because they are, in large part, about understanding human experience and behaviour.

Inevitably learning history and geography will take children beyond their own personal experiences, into other people's perspectives. These will often involve controversy and debate. For example:

- conducting a survey among parents about their shopping habits to explore reliance on local stores versus large supermarkets;
- interviewing a grandparent about their childhood;
- discussing the pros and cons of advertising (needs versus wants);
- hearing about different people's views about a proposed local road by-pass;
- learning about the roles of different people in the school community – and their perspective on the school itself;
- talking to someone who is or who has been on strike;
- participating in a debate about whether we should eat meat.

It seems to me that the humanities both require and foster the approach to life which starts with 'what if?' They demand of learners that they apply imagination to their existing and received representations of life.

I would argue that whichever model or combination of the three models you adopt in teaching the humanities in your own practice, *each* demands the development of imagination and creativity in children. As already hinted at above, the humanities are not value-free.

Values in history and geography

History is an interpretive field: it is about interpreting evidence to piece together events and perspectives of people who, more often than not, lived before our own lifetimes. Historians themselves are working with 'leftovers' from earlier times, and need to exercise both keen observation and analysis, with imagination, to try and understand what different pieces of evidence might be saying about life in an earlier period. Teaching children this central idea involves both imagination and creativity.

Working on actual primary sources may not always be possible, particularly with younger children, but the idea of working with incomplete leftovers can be simulated in the classroom and locality using accessible resources, such as pictures, artefacts, simple written sources, buildings, oral accounts. Theatre, simulation and dramatic play can help children take on the perspectives of people living in different eras, and of different people living in the same era.

It has been argued that history has traditionally been about, and documented by, men, and that the history curriculum in schools is almost exclusively a white, male story. It seems to me that developing creativity in history also means encouraging children to ask questions about this and other assumptions which underly some of the received knowledge which they will meet.

Similarly, until about twenty years ago, the study of geography in schools was far more about the physical side of the subject (mapping skills, geology, patterns in the environment) than about the social. But as the domain of geography itself has evolved, so has the school curriculum so that even with very small children it now incorporates the study of peoples and their impacts on each other and their environments. I would argue, with Edwards and Knight, that

> In a democracy committed to human rights, liberty and equality, intolerance of others is a cause for considerable concern, especially as Britain develops an identity as part of Europe rather than as the leader of many countries . . . geography is important as a *human* subject in a humanistic society.
>
> (Edwards and Knight, 1994: 68)

Although they are referring to the early years primarily, this notion of geography as being a moral study certainly holds with the older years. One of the main concerns of geography has to be about understanding the different perspectives of people living in different places, or belonging to different interest groups in the same place. And it will involve coming to have a sense of what it *feels* like to take on those different perspectives. Feeling, as Mary Warnock (1976) has argued, is absolutely central to imagination.

Summing up: the humanities

I have suggested that the humanities involve imagining different possibilities, offering:

- multiple perspectives on the present and the past (both descriptive and analytical);
- exploration of values and assumptions embedded in 'received' knowledge;
- opportunities for investigating human impact on the environment (other people as well as the wider world, i.e. exploration of the morality of human action).

I have suggested that the National Curriculum for history and geography specifies education about and for these subjects and that the process of educating 'through' them is left in the domain of the teacher.

Summary of Chapter 4

The arts and humanities offer many ways of developing creativity. They can provide bridges with the sciences through sensory experience, visual experimentation and critical analysis. In this chapter I have tried to demonstrate some of the ways in which the arts and humanities play a key role in supporting the development of children's creativity in the primary curriculum.

Acknowledgements

Grateful thanks are due to Annie Clarke, Franny Hughes-Campbell and Harriet Quigley for their pieces of creative writing quoted here.

5 Maths and science

This chapter is concerned with some school subjects which sometimes get ignored in discussions of creativity. I explore here ways in which creativity can be seen as fundamental to maths and science. For each subject, I relate the discussion to the National Curriculum.

Mathematical thinking

Mathematics has a language system of its own, made up of figures and symbols. It is essentially about representing relationships in the world, and manipulating them. It is, therefore, a specific way of thinking. Whether we are talking about number, algebra, shape and space, data handling, etc., each mathematical topic contains a range of basic concepts which, once grasped, can give even very young children access to all kinds of exploration.

The building blocks

We need words, spoken and written, as a tool to help us express our thinking in linguistic parts of the curriculum. Similarly, at any level of mathematics, children need to have learned some of the building blocks, or basic concepts, in order to be able to explore with them.

Even with a very early grasp of a mathematical concept it is possible to begin thinking mathematically, as demonstrated in these two examples from children I have worked with in inner London.

Jessica and Wale, aged 8, were working on some missing number questions which involved creative arithmetic. They each had a list of number statements which were incomplete, and which used all four number rules, for example

$$12 = \underline{} + \underline{}$$
$$12 = \underline{} - \underline{}$$
$$12 = \underline{} \times \underline{}$$
$$12 = \underline{} \text{ divided by } \underline{}$$
$$12 = \underline{} + \underline{} - \underline{}$$
$$12 = \underline{} \underline{} \underline{}$$

Having each found a list of possible number combinations, they compared notes with one another.

Ola, aged 5, was sorting plastic cars and other shapes into sorting hoops. He had been asked to sort 'all the cars and all the green things', and he set out two hoops initially, until he came to a green car which belonged in both hoops. After a long think, he overlapped the sorting hoops and continued. The following day he chose to work in the maths corner during 'choosing' time, and explored sorting with duplo, using a number of different categories, such as 'all the squares and all the blue things', 'all the people and all the cars' and so on. In each case he found that there was at least one piece which belonged in more than one category. By the end of the day he had discovered that he could use a number of sorting hoops at once, and that they could overlap with one another.

Conjecture and confidence

Confidence in our own mathematical thinking can make a big difference to the ways in which we enable children to engage with the subject. In her exploration of primary teachers' attitudes to mathematics, Briggs (1989) has illustrated that our own experiences of learning mathematics often contribute more to the way we feel about the subject, than the actual content. Some of the experiences which she describes as contributing to lack of confidence in the subject are:

- an emphasis on speed of working, with the associated (and false) expectation that mathematicians find answers to problems almost instantly;
- memories of failing;
- for women in particular, the view that mathematics is the domain of males ... and, in recalling their own school days, a perception of their teachers' expectations that boys would find it easy while in contrast girls were less likely to achieve success.

A learning environment which implies that maths involves the clear-cut dichotomies of knowing or not knowing, succeeding or failing, can produce some of these feelings as an outcome. Such a learning atmosphere can lead to learners feeling threatened and exposed. On the other hand, one which values conjecture and possibility, is one which enables everyone to try out their mathematical thinking, with a feeling of 'can-do'.

Conjecture and possibility language in mathematics

An aspect of creating a conjecturing atmosphere is to encourage children to couch their ideas in exploratory terms. For example, 'perhaps if' or 'I suggest that', or 'maybe if' ... In an environment such as this, it is the responsibility not only of the teacher, but of the children as well, to be aware of the differing levels of confidence and knowledge, and to work together to allow everyone to express their ideas at the level that they are able to. You may be able to recall occasions when you have felt a sense of relief when someone else has voiced a question which had been puzzling you also, but which you perhaps felt nervous of asking. A conjecturing atmosphere, where the language of possibility is valued, encourages all children to speak up when they are not certain.

Whichever ways you organise the teaching of maths, whether as a whole-class activity, in small groups or individually, children will engage much more creatively if possibility language is the way in which they voice their thinking.

Published resources and maths activities

Most primary teachers use a published maths scheme as the backbone of their work in this subject. And they do have lots of advantages:

- it is often possible for children to work at an individual pace;
- they can be useful for helping children practise knowledge (such as number bonds or times tables) or techniques (such as the number algorithms, or finding the area of a shape);
- many maths schemes contain mathematical investigations.

As in any subject, however, the scheme and its text books, workbooks and other paraphernalia is only one part of your resources as a teacher. Setting up activities which enable children to investigate either individually or collaboratively, and which involve them applying the basic concepts, is really essential to enable their mathematical thinking.

Enabling mathematical creativity through activities

Activities that generate more than one conjecture provide opportunities for creativity. Enabling children to engage with maths creatively means encouraging them to use maths as a tool, both for its own sake and for some practical purpose, having negotiated some shared understandings as a starting point, as the following example may illustrate.

Ben was helping his class of 6- and 7-year-old children come to recognise features of 3-D shapes. He started by negotiating some shared understandings by using a 'feely bag', along with one of each of the solid shapes in it. The children took turns to have a go at recognising through touch, then naming a shape, and finally withdrawing it from the feely bag to compare with the shapes on display. Doing this meant Ben could encourage the children to think about the relevant criteria – which were to do with the three-dimensionality of the shapes. Using the feely bag was a gentle strategy to help the children learn that other criteria, such as colour and texture, are not relevant in naming a 3-D shape. After doing this activity a few times, Ben encouraged the children to build and therefore experiment with the properties of 3-D shapes by providing lots of shape blocks in the construction area. Later he showed the children how artists and architects can use shape. He set each child a one-day mini project on 3-D shape, which involved identifying a question to find out answers to. The children's projects included 'What is the best way of storing the big and little PE balls?', 'Why are there different patterns of brick in our school wall?' and 'Why don't builders use spheres?' Finding answers to their questions involved a mixture of convergent and divergent thinking.

Activities which enable creativity in maths can also need time and simple practical resources. Most people, adults and children, need concrete evidence for their mathematical thinking, and enough time to first see, then explore, patterns. Representing mathematical thinking through pictures (diagrams, number lines, sets, etc.) and symbols is another way of seeing concrete evidence, as Haylock and Cockburn (1989) demonstrate in their work on early years maths. They argue that it is only having represented their mathematical thinking in some way that children can generalise their ideas about any aspect of maths.

The subject orders for mathematics

The programmes of study for mathematics in the National Curriculum (DfE, 1995f) offer plenty of room for fostering mathematical thinking. A significant part of the curriculum for both Key Stage 1 and Key Stage 2 involves using and applying mathematics and in both key stages this includes developing mathematical language and communication, and developing mathematical reasoning.

The fostering of mathematical thinking, language and exploration is also evident in the other parts of the curriculum for both key stages. For example, the number programme of study for Key Stage 1 requires children to 'develop flexible methods of working with number, orally and mentally', to 'use a variety of practical resources and contexts' and 'record in a variety of ways, including ways that relate to their mental work' (p. 3). Throughout the number part of the programme of study for Key Stage 1, the exploratory language and approach of the curriculum remains evident, so that, for example, children are expected to 'explore and record patterns in addition and subtraction, and then patterns of multiples' (p. 3), to 'sort and classify a set of objects using criteria related to their properties' and to 'collect, record and interpret data . . . using an increasing range of charts, diagrams, tables and graphs' (p. 4). In Key Stage 2, children are expected to 'explore number sequences' and to 'develop a variety of mental methods of computation with whole numbers up to 100' (p. 7), and in solving numerical problems, to 'check results by different methods' (p. 8).

In the shape, space and measures part of the Key Stage 1 curriculum, children are required to 'describe and discuss shapes and patterns that can be seen or visualised' , to 'begin to classify shapes according to mathematical criteria' and to 'compare objects and events using appropriate language' (p. 5). In Key Stage 2, children are required to explore and express geometry, pattern and measures. This includes making 2-D and 3-D shapes and patterns, exploring 'their geometrical features and properties' (p. 9) so that they can be classified, and also solving problems using them. It includes, too, applying their understanding of measures so that they can 'choose appropriate standard units of length, mass, capacity and time, and make sensible estimates with them in everyday situations' (p. 9).

The data handling part of the Key Stage 2 mathematics curriculum involves investigation of their own mathematical questions through statistical means.

Throughout the mathematics curriculum and across the key stages, the use of information technology is encouraged, as both a source of data and a tool for exploring and manipulating it. Later in this chapter I explore information technology as a curriculum area in its own right.

Summing up: maths and creativity

I have suggested that children can be encouraged to use possibility language in order to conjecture in mathematics, within the parameters of their conceptual knowledge. A knowledge of the basics (concepts and language), and fostering confidence in oneself as a teacher, are important if you are to enable children to apply possibility thinking.

I have suggested that activities which enable multiple conjectures encourage children's creativity in mathematics, and that maths schemes, whilst useful for building the basics, should form only a part of the repertoire of resources for supporting the mathematical thinking of children aged 3–13. There are, of course, exceptions; some schemes encourage children to make multiple conjectures.

By brief reference to aspects of the mathematics subject orders in the National Curriculum, I have tried to demonstrate that possibility thinking and investigative language and approaches are embedded within it.

Science and creativity?

While researching this book, I met some teachers who said they felt that science and maths were not creative subjects. In fact, some of the most creative people the world has seen have been mathematicians or scientists, or both. Think of Einstein – or before him, Newton. Or Marie Curie. There is, of course, some considerable difference between the building blocks of the school maths and science curricula, and the level of specialisms at which great scientists or mathematicians operate. Yet I would argue that both maths and science involve and require creativity, even at school level. I have tried to demonstrate this in mathematics in the preceding pages. As to science, if we as teachers feel that this subject is not creative, what kinds of messages are we passing on to children about the subject they are studying?

Representations of science

The notion of the scientist as an inventor seems to be embedded in the ways children (and also many adults) think of science. This is as true of science in the classroom as it is beyond. As Murphy and Scanlon's work (1994) illustrates, when children are asked to draw a picture of a scientist they often draw someone (usually a man) in a white coat, experimenting with strange liquids and long mathematical formulae, in order to invent something, illustrated by the typical picture drawn by Hatty, in Y6 (Figure 5.1). I had asked her to draw me a scientist.

The process of investigation: children as scientists

A large part of science is the process of investigation; itself reflected in the way National Curriculum for science is presented. What I focus on in the next part of this chapter is creativity within the process of scientific investigation.

The process of being a scientist, then, begins with asking questions – the 'what if' and 'why' which as I suggested in Chapters 1 and 2 is at the core of creative thinking – and investigating possible answers to them by planning experiments,

Figure 5.1 A child's drawing of a scientist

obtaining and considering evidence. Turning an idea into a question to ask is the beginning of any investigation.

After finding a question to ask, the rest of the process of planning an experiment or investigation involves:

- making predictions;
- deciding how to test these;
- making a 'fair test';
- deciding how to observe;
- measuring and recording;
- deciding what conclusions can be drawn from the results of the investigation;
- communicating the results.

The end of the process will involve children deciding what new investigations they might want to do. Having said this, the process presented above is an 'educator construct', and children do not always complete all parts of it on all occasions!

All science starts with observation: of phenomena, or properties, of a living being, a process or an inanimate object. A range of basic resources is therefore essential to fostering scientific enquiry in children. In other words, it is important to provide plenty of opportunities for them to observe phenomena or properties, both within the classroom and outside of it. CD-ROM technology now allows a great deal to be brought in to the classroom, on which some observations, if not always investigations, can be based.

Helping children to identify their own questions

Helping children to think of questions which *they* want to find out the answers to is important. They will find it easier and more meaningful to try and find out the answers if they themselves have asked the questions.

One way of enabling children to identify the questions they want to ask is by posing questions which stimulate their thinking. Questions which are closely tied to what the children may be already thinking about are most helpful. The important thing is to develop the children's confidence in their own ideas – and using open questions can help in this.

'Open' questions have lots of possible answers, not just one correct one. They often begin with 'Why' or 'What' or 'How'. For example, 'How can you tell if these things are living?' or 'Why do apples have pips?' or 'How does the dough change when it goes in the oven?' Open questions allow children to voice their own ideas. They also allow you to hear what the children have noticed, and what they consider important. Open questions also encourage children to get involved in the process of investigation.

On the other hand, 'closed' questions are ones where there is one correct answer. Such questions often have a 'Yes' or 'No' answer, or a specific place, description, name or time. They often begin with words like 'Where' or 'When' or 'Is it'. For example, 'Where is the ice now?' or 'When does chocolate melt?' or 'Is the light bulb on?'

In scientific investigation and experimentation, you need to use both open and closed questions. As may be apparent from the examples above, closed questions can help children to observe what is happening. Open questions can help them to work out why that is.

Inevitably, if you are genuinely encouraging children to ask their own questions, they may come up with ones which are simply impossible to investigate in a normal primary classroom (although if you had a science laboratory with specialised equipment it might be possible). And it may not be possible to find any answer at all to some questions! So the discourse of science investigations needs to include recognition of what is, and what is not, possible to follow through in the classroom, whatever age group you are working with. Another strategy is to create structured opportunities for children to ask scientific questions.

The next step from creating the questions is for the children to decide which ones are testable and, from there, how they might test them. This means making predictions.

Supporting the development of children's predictions

You can help young children to make predictions by asking them questions about their investigations. The questions should encourage them to think *what* might happen, not why. The more the children are able to visualise what might happen, the better able they will be to test out their predictions.

Each activity will produce a slightly different mix of reasons for predicting. One of the challenges for the teacher can be how to encourage the children to notice something about their investigation which might help them to predict.

How creative is the rest of the process of scientific investigation?

I have focused so far on asking questions and making predictions, because they are perhaps the most creative part of the process of being a scientist. This is not to say that the other aspects of the process are uncreative. Adopting an atmosphere of conjecture, and by valuing more than one possibility at any stage, whether it is deciding on a way of both testing a hypothesis and interpreting the results of a test, is a way of maintaining creativity throughout a scientific investigation.

Deciding how to test predictions

Children's ideas about how to test their predictions will usually involve trying out them out. A key skill in testing scientific predictions, which most children will develop during the top end of primary school, i.e. during Key Stage 2, is the notion of a fair test. The National Curriculum for Key Stage 1 also specifies that children should be taught to recognise when a comparison or a test is fair or unfair.

To make a fair test, the children need to have worked out the relevant, independent, dependent and control variables. Young children, however, will need lots of help to work out that a fair test is needed, and how to set one up. Few children in Key Stage 1 will be able to cope with the idea of a fair test. Although the thinking involved in devising a fair test may involve convergent, logical thinking, the notion of 'possibility' is at its core. Occasionally, too, a divergent idea can contribute to devising the fair test.

A creative approach to fostering fair testing is one which enables all children to feel their ideas are valued, although eventually the only ones which will be chosen will be those which provide a genuine 'fair test'. There is an inevitable tension between accepting all ideas and deciding upon the most appropriate one; similar to that involved in 'brainstorming' where all ideas are accepted initially, but later they are sifted and a smaller number chosen, on the basis of some shared criteria.

Observation and possibility thinking

Science observation involves focusing attention on factual detail and is supported by questions like 'What can you see?', 'What do you notice?', 'What do you find inside/outside?', 'What do you feel, see, hear, taste?', 'How many, how long, how often?' Observation is also more sharply focused by comparison questions, for example 'In how many ways are your leaves alike and how do they differ?'

Part of the process of becoming a scientist is being able to choose appropriate ways of observing, since science provides a pre-specified way of looking at things. Through 'modelling', children can be introduced powerfully to the kinds of questions they could ask. Although the questions are therefore constrained I would suggest they have at their core the 'what if' of possibility thinking.

Measuring and recording

Measuring is not necessarily involved in every investigation. For example, if children are investigating simple properties of different materials by exploring their textures, appearance, transparency and whether they are magnetic or non-magnetic, they may not need to measure anything. But if they are finding out what happens when water is heated or cooled, they will need to find a way of measuring what is applied to the water and how it responds. Helping children decide what to measure with involves supporting them in learning what each kind of measuring instrument can do.

Measuring instruments which young children might use in science will include ones which they have created for themselves. For instance, in an investigation into the conditions under which seeds grow, the children may devise their own forms of ruler (made up, for example, of finger-widths, Unifix cubes, or from squared paper). Children can sometimes find ways of using their measuring instruments which would not have occurred to you as the adult. This is another aspect of creativity within science.

Discussions about how and what they are measuring will reveal the children's ideas about what the measuring instrument is capable of. This can provide you with opportunities to extend the children's understanding – and to stimulate their creativity.

Recording the outcomes of a science investigation can involve creativity. There are a variety of different ways of recording work from a science investigation. They include drawing, annotated drawings, log books or diaries, writing, creating a bar chart, a graph or a table of results, and even talking in to a tape recorder. Children's personal recordings, in the form of diagrams, notes, spider charts and networks, can help them and you to see each child's connections between the ideas.

The National Curriculum and creativity in science

Although there are several 'content' areas in the National Curriculum subject orders for science, introducing children to the nature of scientific enquiry and of scientific ideas is given strong emphasis. Thus, in Key Stage 1, pupils are to be given opportunities to develop and ask their own questions, to 'use focused exploration and investigation to acquire scientific knowledge, understanding and skills' and 'to relate simple scientific ideas to the evidence for them' (DfE, 1995i: 2). All of these involve children in using possibility thinking, considering 'what if?' in a variety of ways for a range of purposes.

The engine of possibility thinking is evident in the subject orders for Key Stage 2 also, where children are expected, for example, to 'ask questions related to their work in science', to 'use focused exploration and investigation to acquire scientific knowledge, understanding and skills', to 'use their knowledge and understanding of science to explain and interpret a range of familiar phenomena' and to 'obtain evidence to test scientific ideas in a variety of ways' (DfE, 1995i: 7).

It seems to me, then, that science in the National Curriculum both requires and affords possibilities for the development of creative thinking.

Summing up on maths and science

As should be clear from this chapter, both maths and science involve:

- posing questions and exploring answers to them;
- having access to domain-specific knowledge and concepts in order to do so.

The National Curriculum for both subjects makes this explicit, and, I would argue, therefore encourages creative thinking as core to each of the two subjects.

Both involve what is called 'deductive' reasoning (which goes something like this: 'because this has happened I presume that the actions which led to it had such and such a function'). Both involve prediction, based on a body of knowledge. Perhaps because of this, many teachers don't consider these parts of the school curriculum to be creative. However, both involve coming to new understandings and each has its own language which represents thinking.

Both require creativity in that they demand that questions are asked, such as 'what if?' . . .

Concluding thoughts

Einstein said,

Imagination is more important than knowledge.

I am of the view, as I hope I have demonstrated during this chapter, that in maths and science *both* imagination (in the sense of possibility thinking) *and* knowledge (including skill) are important for the children to whom we pass on our world. I want to explore these ideas a little further in the next chapter, which looks at what I would describe as the application of science and maths: technology, including information and communication technology.

Acknowledgements

Thanks are due to my colleagues in The Open University School of Education, for informal conversations and drafting processes over the past eight years, which have informed the writing of this chapter. I have also drawn on material and research for the maths section from the Centre for Mathematics Education in The Open University and for the science section on an early draft of my writing for The Open University's Specialist Teaching Assistants' Course (E660). Thanks also to Hatty Bennett for her drawing of a scientist.

6 Technology: how is it creative?

In this chapter I look at creativity in information and communication technology and in design and technology. I ask, and try to answer, questions such as 'How can a computer offer scope for creativity?' 'How do you foster design and technology as an authentic activity for children in practice?' Finally I look at the social implications of creativity and technology.

Computers and creativity?

I have often come across teachers expressing the view that computers, far from stimulating or fostering creativity, both represent and do the exact opposite of this.

Yet, many of the games which are available for computers, the differentiated learning activities where children can monitor their own levels of achievement, particularly on basic skills like reading or even keyboard skills, and some of the open ended investigations are all ways in which children's creativity can be enhanced by computers.

I would argue that the most powerful contribution that computers make to learning is through communications. Recently, one of my colleagues at The Open University was visiting the School of Education in Milton Keynes, on research leave from his own university in Wagga Wagga, New South Wales, Australia. He was researching in a primary school there, and also in one in England. Since he was the common link, he encouraged children in both schools to write to one another, but not using pencil and paper. Instead, the children sent each other messages through electronic mail. The children in Australia also sent messages to him whilst he was here in England. The communication was thus inter-generational and inter-cultural too; the children had lots of questions about what he was doing on his visit, what he had seen and who he had met. If it weren't for the time difference between the two countries, the children and my colleague could have 'talked' to each other through the e-mail system in 'real time' rather than waiting until the next day for a response to their messages. Instead, they chatted through electronic mail waiting a day or so at a time to get a response to each previous comment or question.

As I hope this example has shown, computers can provide a technology for fostering relationships in new ways, and transcending geographical and cultural boundaries.

They also provide a source of and a tool for manipulating information, as Hammond has argued (1988). Take, for example, spreadsheets. A spreadsheet allows you to make calculations very fast in order to model possible outcomes as variables are altered. For example, if I am working out how much it will cost to produce an Open University course or pack, I have to think about various different costs: the writing costs if we use a consultant, the editing, the design, the printing, the warehousing, the postage and distribution. Each of these costs varies with the amount of material involved. So, for each additional page, it costs more to write, edit and design. But printing in bulk costs much less per page than printing a small quantity. And, of course, that is just the print – it doesn't include video, audio cassettes, CD-ROMs, etc. So the calculations are quite complicated. If I want to work out what we should charge students to study the course, I need to build in other costs, such as staff time for briefing and looking after tutors, tutor time for teaching the course face to face, and so on. Rather than having to work all of the possible variations out by hand, I can create a spreadsheet. What is really exciting about spreadsheets is that as the user you are in charge of how they make the calculations! So, I can make up a plan for my spreadsheet to multiply, for example, the unit cost of each page of editing by the number of pages which I anticipate, and to multiply the unit cost of design per page to the number of pages which I anticipate, and so on – and to add all of the outcomes together at the end. Making up the algebraic equations which drives that function is a creative process: there are often a number of different equations, each of which refers to a different part of the production process. So I need to develop an equation which will find out the total cost of each item, and then an overarching one which will total all of the functions at the end. Children, by the top end of junior school, are quite capable of setting up spreadsheets for their own purposes.

Adventure games provide another set of possibilities for children because although the worlds which they can explore are in fact predetermined by the programme, they are often very complex, with events, characters, problems to be solved, and some kind of 'quest'. These kinds of games can provide stimulus for imagination at all kinds of levels. Some games are presented as simulations, such as diving to retrieve a Tudor shipwreck, or having conversations with Egyptian priests in order to identify an object found on an archaeological dig. There are, of course, problems with the assumptions which can be implied by such simulations, as Scaife and Wellington (1993) point out: in real life the variables cannot be controlled with such ease, so the picture which is presented may be misleading. In addition, it is possible, as with any account, to come across biased CD-ROM presentations which, on the face of it, close down creativity. But given a critically reflective environment, even biased accounts can be used to stimulate creative responses in children.

Another creative capability which computers can help develop is the use of control technology through robots and programmes such as LOGO. The children can actually make up the instructions which control the movement of the turtle, robot or whatever. In this way computers become what Turkle and Papert (1990) call tools to think with.

Another way in which computers can engage with individual creativity, as Loveless (1995) has pointed out, is their ability to present data in a wide variety of ways. These include using sound, colour and movement. Cartoon-like animation, displaying information in the form of graphs and charts, or in the form of 3-D models, means that children whose dominant learning styles need information in visual, auditory or modelled form are much better provided for. Because the child controls the pace at the touch of a button, there is scope for stretching each child's cognitive abilities.

The accessing of information through computers, then, has specific features. Essentially, the information provided via a computer is non-linear. In other words, not organised in a follow-on fashion in the way that, for example, a book is set out, but rather set out as layers of options through a branching structure, which can be accessed in an order chosen by the user.

Accessing non-linear information

Non-linear information contrasts with linear information where the order of presentation is much more predefined. Linear information may include more than one form of material (e.g. story tapes or, for adult learners, Open University-style materials). The point is that the actual process of accessing non-linear information offers plenty more opportunities for creative thinking than information which is presented in linear form. Consider this example:

Alan and Christine are both class teachers in the same primary school, which provides each classroom with two computers, some of which have CD-ROM facilities. They have, however, very different approaches to learning with information technology.

Christine, who is the IT co-ordinator, has a class of 32 children in Y5. She decided to use a CD-ROM package and a database programme as resources for the children in exploring Tudor England. The children worked in threes on the computer in timetabled slots throughout the day. She divided the history topic in half. In the first half, she provided the children with some information about the topic, through:

- the CD-ROM which the children could search themselves;
- a dramatic play during one whole school assembly (by a local theatre-in-education style group);
- a visit to a local museum;
- a variety of source books borrowed from a local library;
- some direct teaching in the classroom.

As they gathered information she asked the children to work in a variety of ways to identify questions which they wished to know answers to, concerning the period under study. The children's questions were then pooled and refined by the class to a manageable number.

In the second half of the history topic, the children were to find out answers to a variety of questions agreed by the class. She also added a few of her own. The resources included the CD-ROM, further library searches and also the database.

Alan, on the other hand, teaches 33 children in Y6. Although the children are even more capable of the kind of work Christine's class was undertaking, he is not keen on computers. Since Christine works with his class once a fortnight for an afternoon whilst he takes her class for maths, he tends to leave the IT to her. In contrast he teaches the Victorians from a text book, which both defines and answers the questions which might be asked about that era. As the book was published after the most recent National Curriculum Orders and there are enough for the children to share one between two, he sees no problem in working through it chapter by chapter on a Tuesday afternoon, supplemented by direct classroom teaching, a visit to the museum, a walk around the locality looking at Victorian houses and a story-time book based on the adventures of three Victorian children.

There are a number of differences in their teaching styles, but one of the most significant is that because Alan is using linear sources much more heavily, the nature of his children's enquiry into their history topic involves them in less personal definition and selection of knowledge.

Computer-aided learning often involves the learner choosing the order in which they wish to access information. You may have observed children using CD-ROM disks of encyclopaedias or museums, for example. The child can decide what they want to find out about, and when. They may also decide how they want to find out (i.e. through screen text, on-screen video, computer audio or through the graphics, or a combination of all). The introduction of this kind of choice is highly significant, as researchers on both sides of the Atlantic are finding out. As CD-ROM in particular becomes a more widespread medium for storing a variety of information (sound, images, text), we may predict that the assumption that a user can find their way through a non-linear menu of possibilities will become a natural part of the expectations on young children for learning, both in school and at home. And as the Internet and WWW become more available to the general public, including children, this need for non-linear processing skills will increase.

As teachers we need to be aware of what the medium of instruction expects of the child. This argument is made by an American review team (Alexander, Kulikowich and Jetton, 1994) who have published a summary of sixty-six studies by diverse researchers in education in this arena. I would argue that we also need to be aware of what opportunities are offered by each medium, for problem finding and problem solving. My perspective here is that the more scope there is for children to define their own questions, i.e. to problem-find, the more scope the medium offers for creativity.

Of course, we need to be aware of potential barriers which can exist for both children and teachers in using information and communication technology.

Aside from needing to develop skills of being able to decode non-linear information, some people do find computers impersonal, and even, as Alan in the case study above puts it, 'irrelevant'! There is also evidence that gender may play a part in how accessible the technology actually is (Spender, 1995).

On the other hand, information and communication technology can offer access to people who have found it difficult to learn through linear and word-based models. Take, for example, dyslexics. There are now computer programmes which, operating on voice-recognition, can help someone who simply cannot read or write with any fluency to write on to the screen. Tom West's (1991) work on visual learners and dyslexia suggests that computers can offer alternative ways of representing complex issues through three-dimensional, visual models.

Finally, computers offer a tool for creating works of art. For example, it is possible to paint and draw using them, investigating and trying out many possibilities in a way which is not possible when using the 'wet' materials. Information and communication technology can enable composers to play music which they hear in their heads and for that sound automatically to generate a written musical score. This enables a composer who hears their music to short-circuit the arduous process of creating the score.

Learning activities and authenticity

There is increasing evidence that a vital aspect of effective learning activities is that they are authentic (i.e. meaningful) for pupils. This is one reason why communicating through electronic mail works as a creative learning medium for some people – they genuinely want to find out what is happening in someone else's life, or to hear about someone else's ideas.

There is another sense in which learning needs to be authentic: in the sense of being situated within a subject area. For learning in any part of the curriculum involves to some extent at any rate what Clayden *et al.* (1994) call 'enculturation' – in other words, learning the culture of a particular domain. An implication for teaching and learning is that children need clear and explicit access to the subjects of the curriculum themselves and not just to their packaging. So, children need access to the culture of the information stored on the hard disk, floppy disks and CD-ROMs, just as they need access to the culture and 'rules' of reading books. AND they also need access to the culture of the subject which the computer programme, game, etc. is about.

It follows then that teachers need a good knowledge of the 'culture' of a domain of knowledge in order to assess and plan children's learning so that it is authentic. So, in the case study given earlier in this chapter, Christine needed a good knowledge of the culture of the domain of history and historical study. Alan put a lot of trust in the text book, the museum and his knowledge of local architecture to provide an appropriate model for using and interpreting evidence. By relying on a fewer range of sources and by relying quite heavily on the text book, Alan simplified his own preparation and thinking. On the other hand, he offered the children fewer opportunities to explore authentic aspects of the subject, and limited the extent to which they could practise the skills of the historian. There were also few opportunities for creative, generative thinking.

The National Curriculum, computers and creativity

As we would expect, computers, or 'information technology', the term in common currency when the most recent National Curriculum was published (1995), are a requirement of each subject of the curriculum – in other words, pupils are to be given opportunities to develop their computer skills as appropriate in each subject. In addition, information technology itself is identified as a separate curriculum area. Computers are seen as a tool and as a source of information in the way the curriculum is written, as indicated in the following:

> Information technology (IT) capability is characterised by an ability to use effectively IT tools and information sources to analyse, process and present information, and to model, measure and control external events. This involves:
>
> - using information sources and IT tools to solve problems;
> - using IT tools and information sources, such as computer systems and software packages, to support learning in a variety of contexts,
> - understanding the implications of IT for working life and society. (DfE, 1995e: p. 1)

This last part of the quotation is important, as it implies that children and teachers are to use their imaginations about the consequences of information technology for society as a whole. I have argued earlier that imagination is essential for creative thinking.

The wording of the National Curriculum for information technology suggests an emphasis on pupil autonomy in thinking, not merely in operating the technology. I would argue that the other parts of the IT capability statement given above also demand creativity of pupils; for solving problems and using IT tools and information sources each require a questioning approach about what might be appropriate – in other words, possibility thinking. And as indicated in Chapter 1, this approach is the core of creative thinking.

Summing up: information and communication technology

As computers foster both communication and information, it seems appropriate that the term 'information and communication technology' has been developed for this medium over the last few years. I have suggested that computers, used as a communication tool, both foster and stimulate creativity, by fostering relationships whilst transcending geographic boundaries. Although computers are indeed a source of stored information and in that sense not creative at all, they also offer tools for possibility thinking (and therefore creativity) in both interpreting and communicating that data. This is in part because data can be accessed in a non-linear fashion – and following the thinking of the interrogator. I have discussed three different kinds of computer-based activity designed for children which I believe foster creativity: adventure games, open-ended investigations and control technology.

One of the challenges to enabling children's capability in being creative with computers is the need to become 'enculturated' within the culture of the ICT medium. That can be challenging for teachers who themselves do not feel drawn in. In addition, activities need to be as 'authentic' as possible, so that children's learning does not feel to them like 'cold' exercises which may be disconnected from their interests.

Finally I have discussed the 1995 National Curriculum for information technology, which it seems to me demands imagination and creativity of pupils and their teachers.

Design and technology

Design and technology has at its core the need for children to think creatively: to experiment, to be open to possibility, to take risks, to be prepared to combine old ways of seeing with new ones, to be prepared to look at a situation or problem in different ways, to seek innovation, to be resourceful.

It also requires both 'right and left brain thinking', as introduced in Chapter 1. Design and technology requires, in other words, intuition, spatial orientation, crafts, skills, emotions, expression (all right hemisphere operations) as well as language, sequencing, logic and mathematical operations. I would argue that it is particularly important to give children space to access the right hemisphere's functions, by offering opportunities to generate and clarify ideas through working together, through drama, discussion, also modelling, sketching, painting, working with construction kits, and through information technology drawing and designing packages.

Drawing on its research into design and technology in schools, the Assessment of Performance Unit (APU, 1991; SEAC, 1991) has concluded that key elements are active capability and reflective capability. Cross (1994) has developed these to include creative capability:

Active capability: constructive thinking, doing, action
Reflective capability: evaluating, review
Creative capability: imagination, invention; including aesthetic and technological creativity

(Cross, 1994: 19)

Children's ideas can be stimulated by what the Design and Technology in Education Project (1990) has called 'design awareness'. This means experiencing and engaging critically with the made world of places, products and images. For one of the challenges faced by teachers is how to get a balance between offering children only adult perceptions of the world, and encouraging children to construct their own perceptions without reference to existing cultural norms. As Tickle (1990: 112) puts it, 'the problem faced by the teacher is how to stimulate and guide without imposing too many preconceptions and stereotypes, and without stifling the child's own creativity and logical thinking and making'. At issue then, is how to provide possibilities for children's thinking without pre-constraining their frameworks of reference.

In this sense, as others have argued (Ritchie, 1995), design and technology requires teachers to exercise imagination. The provision of authentic starting points and background contexts for children requires designing the curriculum and activities in a way which allows for many possibilities. Drawing on contexts and experiences which are meaningful to the children requires possibility thinking on the part of the teacher. Clearly, children themselves can identify starting points for investigations which are meaningful to them. Consider the case of Helen.

Helen taught Y6 in an inner city school in Newcastle-upon-Tyne in the early 1990s. She had a policy of seeking children's interests and conceptions at the start of each project of work. When I visited her, the children were undertaking a history project based around the Newcastle Quayside (a historic dockside area which has now become a bijoux place full of craft shops, tea rooms, restaurants and wine bars). As a starting point she asked the children to work first individually and then in small groups to brainstorm and then 'concept map' what they knew about the Quayside, and what questions arose for them about it.

The children reported back to one another in a variety of ways, and from the discussions which followed Helen was able to plan a range of potential starting points for the children. Her expectation, which she shared quite explicitly with the children, was that as their interests developed so too might the topic.

Helen's work demonstrates that opportunities for design and technology exist in lots of curriculum areas and topic focused themes; they also exist in the day-to-day life of the classroom, as the list suggested by Cross (1994) illustrates: 'for example, the storage of coats; the care of pets; the storage of resources; the transport of materials; the library; the gardens and grounds; jobs done in school, etc.' Other sources of starting points for design and technology include the media and children's fiction.

I hope that I have shown through Helen's work that finding out the children's perspectives on what is relevant is possible, as well as important.

Authentic activities

Authenticity is as much an issue in design and technology as it is in information and communication technology. This is so both at policy level, for curriculum designers, and at classroom level too, for teachers.

To examine briefly the policy level first, it has been argued (APU, 1993; Siraj-Blatchford, 1996) that the National Curriculum for design and technology describes a linear model where each stage is clearly defined and distinct from the next. This is an 'ideal-type', in that the actual complex realities of the process of designing, making and evaluating are ignored. Indeed, within the initial version of the National Curriculum for design and technology even the numbering of the attainment targets implied that there was a natural starting point ('Identification of Needs and Opportunities'), which is not necessarily where the design and technology process starts. The linear model is also too difficult for children who are very young or who have very little experience. Identifying a need, or a 'problem' to be solved, requires powers of analysis which, like the creativity required for the design process, do not necessarily spring 'naturally' from within, but rather, need practice in the form of experience and examples from more experienced designers.

Turning now to the classroom, having a 'model' of what is involved in design and technology in your head is important as an underpinning to planning and assessing learning. Ideally, models of the process involved in design and technology should involve children in finding a variety of design solutions to problems which are, increasingly with age and experience, identified by them. But in practice the problem with such models (including the National Curriculum one) is that the approach can become formulaic and artificial. It can stifle creativity because children look for the right answer rather than the optimum solution. And it can make the process of designing and making appear to be smooth and clear. In fact as the APU's research (APU, 1991; SEAC, 1991) carried out between 1985 and 1991 suggests, the process is muddled – children seem to generate ideas and try them out without formal design stages, and they seem to focus on the detail of their ideas. The APU and others (Cross, 1994) describe the muddle of going to and fro between the mind and the hand, or between active and reflective work as a natural part of the process.

Oversimplification may lead on to another problem, in terms of what both teacher and children will accept as 'counting'. McCormick and Davidson (1996) describe research work with children aged 11–14 in which they discovered the teacher highly rated neat work which did not function in practice, over less tidy work which actually did function! This often led to children aiming to please the teacher by producing neat diagrams and drawings, which were, however, non-functional designs!

Technology and play

As I hope has become clear during the second part of this chapter, to some extent design and technology involves creativity, since it is concerned with children realising their own ideas. As well as design and technology being at heart a creative domain, children must use creative forms of expression, such as drawing and other modelling techniques, to explore their thoughts.

Play, too, can be useful as a process to support design and technology (Siraj-Blatchford, 1996). Play can enable children to explore their environment, it can provide opportunities for them to experiment, in other words to go beyond what any object or phenomenon can do, to find out what they can do with it. And finally play can help children to think abstractly, as play objects are representational of the 'real' world. These three approaches to play are drawn from Pepler's (1982) classification of play theories.

Technology, ethics and the future

A driving force, of course, behind design and technology, is that the solution should function. In his writing about divergent thinking, de Bono (1982) emphasises that a way of evaluating the success of an idea is the extent to which it works. But I want to add an ethical dimension also.

Children are the next guardians of our globe, and they take on this role at many levels. The ideas which they have about what to design and make in it will have environmental, economic, social and spiritual impact in the world. It is important that children's ideas function, but more importantly than that, it seems to me, they need the opportunity to explore the implications of choices and ideas. As Einstein said, 'The problems that we face today cannot be solved with the same level of understanding we had when we created them.'

Children need access not only to the processes of inventiveness and innovation, but also familiarity with a critical and ethical framework with which they can evaluate the potential impacts of their inspirations and choices.

Design and technology and the National Curriculum

In many ways design and technology is a creative subject, in that it requires that children design and make products. It combines the generation and combination of ideas with the skills of executing them. These include problem finding as well as problem solving.

Take, for example, part of the programme of study for Key Stage 1 (DfE, 1995e), which specifies the following designing skills:

a) draw on their own experience to help generate ideas;
b) clarify their ideas through discussion;
c) develop their ideas through shaping, assembling and rearranging materials and components;

d)   develop and communicate their design ideas by making freehand drawings, and by modelling their ideas in other ways . . . ;

e)   make suggestions about how to proceed;

f)   consider their design ideas as these develop, and identify strengths and weaknesses.

(DFE, 1995e: 2)

These seem to me to encompass possibility thinking as well as other skills. Similarly, take this extract from the programme of study for Key Stage 2 (DfE, 1995), which includes the following designing skills:

b)   generate ideas, considering the users and purposes for which they are designing;

c)   clarify their ideas, develop criteria for their designs and suggest ways forward . . . ;

e)   explore, develop and communicate aspects of their design proposals by modelling their ideas in a variety of ways;

f)   develop a clear idea of what has to be done, proposing a sequence of actions, and suggesting alternative methods of proceeding if things go wrong;

g)   evaluate their design ideas as these develop, bearing in mind the users and the purposes for which the product is intended, and indicate ways of improving their ideas.

(DFE, 1995e: 4)

Although the emphasis here is perhaps more on critical and analytical thinking than creative thinking, again possibility is present in many of these skills.

Throughout the programmes of study for both key stages, understanding of the domain from which the skills flow is emphasised. This is in keeping with the model of creativity which I introduced in Chapter 2, as involving people, processes and domains.

Summing up: design and technology

I have suggested that design and technology offers a variety of opportunities for creativity, for at its core is the need for children to think creatively and to try out ideas. It requires the use of both 'right and left brain thinking' – introduced in Chapter 1.

In the classroom, design and technology requires teachers to be imaginative for children also need to understand some of the physical properties of materials and tools, and ways of using them, in order to realise their ideas. They also need to engage critically with the made world. Providing authentic learning experiences for children in design and technology depends on an accurate definition of the school curriculum for design and technology, and on teachers having an adequate understanding of criteria for supporting and assessing children's efforts.

I have tried to demonstrate how design and technology provides opportunities for both finding and solving problems, and I have argued that part of a creative approach to design and technology means providing children with access to an ethical framework for evaluating possibilities.

I have suggested that the National Curriculum for design and technology invites and requires creativity, in particular in the programme of study for designing skills.

Part III

Personal and professional development

7 Understanding self and creative potential

In this chapter, I examine aspects of teacher identity, and what may be involved in nourishing the educator. I explore the notion of 'relationship' in teaching and learning, and the role of culture in fostering creativity.

Teacher identity

There is a significant and growing literature concerned with teacher identity. I propose to look at aspects of creative teachers before going on to explore the values which are commonly identified in research concerned with the way teachers see themselves and their role.

Creative teachers are often 'person-orientated' in their attitudes and values. This is well documented by Marilyn Fryer (1996). In her study of 1,028 teachers in the UK, she found that the top ten attitudes which distinguished the most orientated to creativity from those least orientated to it, were:

- wishing to deepen learners' understanding of the world;
- believing all pupils can be creative;
- striving to differentiate teaching for each pupil;
- aiming for learners to respond with empathy;
- valuing pupil self-expression, and teaching skills which facilitate this;
- aiming for pupils to think intuitively;
- valuing free expression work by learners;
- striving to broaden learners' awareness of the world;
- wanting pupils to be able to express their feelings;
- valuing pupils' ideas and questions in assessing creativity.

(adapted from Fryer, 1996)

Indeed, in general, there is evidence, although pre-National Curriculum, that many teachers of young children enter teaching because of their positive regard for other people, particularly children, over and above their interest in the subjects they are to teach (Book, Byers and Freeman, 1983). Person orientation in educators is also a finding in my own research (1996b, 1997) which is post-National Curriculum with its heavy subject bias. Given this, I would expect to find that even teachers trained since the introduction of the National Curriculum, with all the subject-content stipulations which go with initial teacher training, were influenced more in their choice of career by people than by the curriculum subjects.

In a recent book (Craft *et al.*, 1997), I have drawn a distinction between *person-centred teaching* and the set of values which indicate person orientation, because 'person-centred teaching' highlights the people in the learning process above the curriculum. It is similar to the notion of 'unconditional personal regard' which is used in counselling. I have argued that person-centred teaching and learning does not mean disregarding the curriculum, nor does it mean adopting any one particular teaching style, but rather bearing in mind all of the time that at the heart of any classroom activity is learning, for understanding, which is 'owned' by a learner.

Several recent studies have suggested that primary teachers place very high value on the needs of the children they teach. For many teachers this can involve considerable disregard for their own needs as people and as teachers. Teachers, particularly of young children, have been shown to have a strong social/caring orientation (Acker, 1995; Woods, 1990, 1993, 1995; Woods and Jeffrey, 1996; Pollard, 1987; Nias, 1989). They are often very hard working and very busy (Fryer and Collings, 1991; Craft, 1996a). And, as Heather-Jane Robertson's work suggests, discussed by Craft (1996a), this could reflect gender and/or the demands of the job (or a mixture of demands, such as the job plus other family responsibilities) just as much as personal characteristics.

The feeling of 'being there' for the children, of the work never being complete, of one's own needs as irrelevant except insofar as they directly impact meeting the perceived needs of the children is very common and manifests itself as feelings of guilt (Hargreaves and Tucker, 1991). As a relatively recent first-time mother, it occurs to me that there could be a parallel in the way parents (perhaps particularly mothers, or primary carers) see themselves. But to return to primary teachers, one of our biggest challenges, it seems to me, in fostering the creativity of learners is knowing and nourishing oneself.

Knowing and nourishing oneself

In developing strategies for matters such as mentoring, or fostering creativity, then, we often forget to think about ourselves as teacher, our needs and wants.

Knowing oneself is challenging. It may mean accepting a divergence between what one needs and what is possible in terms of external structures; it can also mean looking closely to see to what extent one is creating one's own 'judges and critics', and, therefore, the barriers (Craft, 1998).

Knowing and nourishing oneself also means acknowledging feelings in professional life and development. It potentially allows professional self-study to have an impact on self-esteem. As Marian Dadds (1993, 1995) puts it, 'studying our professional work may mean studying aspects of our daily life which run close to our hearts . . . the more attached we are to our work . . . the more likely it may be that our feelings will be closely implicated'. Teachers involved in my recent study (Craft, 1996b) said they felt that knowing oneself was extremely challenging, since their role as a teacher was to provide, and they had tended to think of their own needs as irrelevant.

Drawing on one of my recent research projects, involving educators in the south-east of England, I would argue that knowing and nourishing oneself as an educator in any domain is critical to being able to provide for others. This is because genuine relationship, with oneself and with others, is at the heart of the process of creativity. The project outcomes described below were the result of an investigation which followed eighteen educators from a range of teaching contexts, from schools to youth work, all of whom had signed up for a post-graduate, professional development course designed to enable them in fostering learner creativity.[1]

During the project we discovered a number of themes which the educators held to be important. An underpinning belief of the group was that for the educator to be creative, s/he needs to be nourished. For the educators in our project, nourishment included taking time for personal development. They had a positive attitude toward their own personal nourishment and were much less focused on the practical questions of, for example, legitimation (within the curriculum structure), resourcing (time, materials, equipment, energy), support (colleagues, critical agent, critical others, receptive pupil culture). In contrast, Woods has documented these as being very important to teachers whom he worked with (1995). The educators in our project began instead from a position of belief in 'creativity as a good thing' regardless of these contextual issues.

But as indicated earlier, taking time for personal nourishment doesn't come easily to teachers as a group. Hard-working, caring, conscientious and self-effacing in many ways, teachers as a profession tend to put the needs of learners in front of their own wants. In our research group, there was a theme of personal and/or professional change having moved individuals to take this particular postgraduate course. For many (ten, i.e. over half) of the group they had reached some kind of a crossroads, or had experienced some kind of 'critical incident' which had influenced their choice to emphasise their study of creativity. Sometimes, critical incidents can be a powerful way of making a change. Here is how one educator put their decision to enrol on the course:

> I suppose because of all the stuff that's going on for me at work and personally at the moment I am very aware of the feelings of getting squashed that happen when you don't get the support . . . you don't get the recognition . . . you don't get the enabling that you want from a particular route . . . so I . . . thought to myself . . . let's go for it.

Another teacher put it like this:

> The course has come . . . at a particular rather vibrant period of my life and I am in the process of change . . . last year I made the sort of bold step to actually claim some of the creativity I knew I ought to be working on by doing a big play [at school] and that taught me quite a lot . . . that plus a personal situation has opened up how I see my immediate future.

For several other teachers the bad experience of Ofsted had motivated them to enrol on the creativity course, as a basis for re-focusing their professional artistry. I use the word artistry to emphasise their experience of contrast between the complex *craft* of teaching and the professional identity which goes with that, compared with their experience of Ofsted (which seemed to de-professionalise their work to much more of a technician-type approach). This theme, of Ofsted inspection experience pushing teachers to 'reclaim' lost parts of their professional life, is one which has been well documented by, among others, Jeffrey and Woods (1998).

Of course, the decision to nourish oneself does not result purely or even necessarily from experiencing some kind of critical incident. But I would argue that it is probably something which one needs to enter into with intention, so one can monitor the extent to which one succeeds. It has been argued that the act of 'choosing' is a key part of being creative (Fritz, 1943).

Being motivated to find ways of nourishing yourself is likely to involve a mixture of personal and professional reasons, although it may involve more of one than the other. One teacher in the project told us that she needed to do lots of craft activities (such as hat-making and dress-making) in her spare time, as that provided a source of inspiration for her. Another decided she wished to travel, so cleared a short space so that she could do so. Another realised he didn't take enough exercise in the countryside any more, and committed to having a long walk at least once a week with his partner. Professional examples of nourishment included a teacher in a management position wanting to develop her creativity by getting some kind of peer supervision and feedback, also a primary teacher wanting to feel some 'ownership' over his job after an Ofsted inspection, rather than feeling controlled and pressured from statutory bodies outside of the school.

During the project we discovered a number of themes which the educators held to be important. An underpinning belief of the group was that for the educator to be creative, s/he needs to be nourished. For the educators in our project, this included taking time for personal development. They each had a positive attitude toward their own personal nourishment and were willing to work around the practical questions of, for example, legitimation (within the curriculum structure), resourcing (time, materials, equipment, energy), support (colleagues, critical agent, critical others, receptive pupil culture). In contrast, Woods (1995) has documented these as being very important challenges and, at times, barriers to teachers whom he worked with. The educators in our project began instead from a position of belief in 'creativity as a good thing' regardless of these contextual issues.

What nourishes the educator?

Within our particular project, the teachers talked of a number of experiences which they found nourishing. These included:

- emotional support;
- being part of a student network;
- getting feedback on their skills and general personal presentation (written and oral) away from but linked with their normal teaching and learning situation; and
- the challenge of studying at MA level.

Some of the teachers worked in the same school. Most of the teachers in that group got a great deal from studying and developing together, although one said they would have preferred a bit more distance.

The responses of our teacher group were specific to the sort of project in which they had chosen to be engaged. There are, of course, many other forms of nourishment than studying for an experiential-based MA level course. For some people, working in a conducive environment is key. It may be out-of-school activities which nourish you; a sport perhaps, or going to hear live music, travelling, or going to the theatre, or seeing friends and family, or reading. The list is endless. To choose appropriate nourishment for yourself means knowing – or sensing – what it is that you need.

What is important, it seems to me, is the intentional act of choice. In Chapter 9, I explore professional development implications of choosing nourishment in order to foster the creativity of learners.

Choosing a creative path

I take the view that creativity is dispositional and not a matter of ability. In other words, that choosing a creative path in any given situation is less a matter of ability to do so and more about 'mind-set' or attitude. Being creative means being inclined to be, and being sensitive to opportunities in which to be so. This is a perspective adopted by Perkins and his colleagues at Project Zero at Harvard University (Perkins, Jay and Tishman, 1993). They argue that ability to be creative is the third aspect of being creative, but that the habit of being inclined to creative behaviour and the quality of alertness, or sensitivity, to opportunities for creative behaviour are just as important.

As Fritz (1943) says, being in the creative orientation means being willing to make choices, and to break the tension between the 'now' and 'possibility'. As an example, one teacher we worked with felt that getting feedback from her colleagues was very important as a source of nourishment. So although she felt a bit shy about doing it, she suggested setting up a peer-mentoring system with one colleague in particular. They called it a 'critical friendship'. In telling us about it she said:

We have tried it before but this term we have made it more formal and divide the time between ourselves and we have a kind of informal contract to both give encouragement but also to challenge each other . . . that really fascinates me as a process because it's very creative.

And making choices can feel like, or actually involve, taking a risk. Through risk comes change, and change is at the core of growth and development. I explore some aspects of taking risks within professional development in Chapter 9.

Self-esteem and creativity

A powerful theme in our own research was the belief that self-esteem and self-confidence must be nourished in order to be creative. This applied to educators as well as to learners. Concern with esteem reflects the social and caring orientation of our particular research group, who in this respect were typical of educators as others have documented (Collings, 1978; Fryer and Collings, 1991; Acker, 1995; Hargreaves and Tucker, 1991; Hargreaves, 1994). In Chapter 9, I discuss a range of practical strategies for professional and personal development which essentially involve ways of nurturing the self-esteem of the educator.

Professional autonomy whilst working with others

Many teachers in the project told us that they needed personal autonomy, and to feel comfortable with their own 'artistry' as an educator (the idea of artistry is explored in several of the chapters of this book including Chapters 2, 6 and 9). The teachers in our project expressed the need to feel able to be 'themselves' as professionals, rather than playing a role ascribed to them by others' expectations. One teacher even described the feeling of exposure and vulnerability which he experienced when unable to have professional autonomy as being 'akin to the removal of trousers'.

What may underlie this expressed need for 'autonomy' in the teaching situation is the scope it gives the impulsive, creative 'Me' to surface more readily, without the judgement/social control of the 'I'. The ambivalence of primary teachers to working with others has been well documented by Nias (1989).

But working with others is a key aspect of teaching, whether one is teaching in a one-to-one situation or in a school with classes of up to 35. Relating and 'being in relationship' with colleagues and with children are central to all that happens in a teaching and learning situation.

Being in relationship

'Relationship' was a major theme emerging from our project. Almost all of the educators involved in it said they valued highly the notion of 'being in relationship'. This was not defined solely in terms of teacher/pupil; teaching and learning were characterised as roles which could be undertaken, and thus the learner sometimes became the teacher and vice versa. Many talked of creativity involving 'being in relationship', meaning that dynamic interaction, with oneself or others or both, is essential to the creative process, whatever domain it might be happening in.

Several talked of empathising with learners. One said 'it's about responding to where they are at and I think that can be quite creative . . . you pitch in as to where they are coming from, you automatically click into a game of under-standing . . . you are trying to stand in their shoes all the time basically' . . . , and another said 'I think it is sometimes just picking up what has meaning for the children.' Talking of how she might approach sex education with her own daughter, one educator said, 'I would find a way of finding out where she is at so that I can communicate with her on that level. Now for me that's being pretty creative.'

Others commented on how different aspects of their lives felt fragmented, and how bringing these parts together through 'self-acknowledgement' felt essential to creative action with others – 'becoming a connected person' as one participant said, 'rather than being disjointed and unconnected which is what a lot of us walk around being'. A youth worker expressed it like this: 'In people I work with [I aim to] develop their uniqueness and their emotion, although I try to do that all the time, I think I could do that better if I know myself more.' An LEA advisor described his need to bring together his home and work selves: 'it's actually getting in touch with your own creativity and the roots of it and the sources of it and trying to work it in, in a vocational sense, into one's job . . . the creative part of me and the work part of me, they are doing this . . . [gestures that they are travelling separate routes and are disconnected].' These comments demonstrate the Assagiolian notion of the transcendent self bringing together aspects of the unconscious self (Assagioli, 1974).

'Being in relationship' also extended to interaction with all constituencies involved in fostering creative action (i.e. other colleagues, learners, parents, other agencies). For example, a governor trainer said: "I need to . . . make people aware . . . and not just the teachers and not just the governors and not just the children but the parents, that as a partnership . . . [all of those] agencies . . . are involved in the education of the person.' This notion of creating with others, or of 'co-creating', is one which seems to appeal to some individuals over and above creating alone. It is important to acknowledge variation in individual style however; not all creative people like to work with others, as some of the literature on 'high' creativity suggests. For example, the work of Csikszentmihalyi (1996) on individuals with high creativity suggests, for many, an intense absorption with and individual focus on the process of creating, without reference to others.

In our study, 'relationship' as a component of creativity extended to the need for audience. This was sometimes expressed at the level of what they themselves needed in order to be creative; one person recognised their own need for an audience – and another felt that what was created was in dynamic relationship with the creator: 'the creating and the created have consciousness and being about each other so there is relationship [and audience] right from the minute the impulse begins.' Another felt that 'you yourself have a relationship with the subject [you are teaching] . . . so you bring energy in with you . . . creativity is shaping energy . . . I think we associate creativity with the idea of bringing a lot of yourself to it.'

Most educators also commented on the *quality* of the teacher/learner relationship. Several educators commented on the need for a good relationship with learners 'before you start anything too experimental . . . So that . . . they know where your borders are before you start' (infant teacher). Many said how much they enjoyed being 'in relationship' with learners, as this comment from an FE lecturer shows: 'I think what nourishes me is . . . the students, I am nourished by students' feedback', and this comment from a primary teacher: 'I think the kids keep me going to be honest . . . I enjoy it, I enjoy being with the kids, they give me a buzz', and from this infant teacher: 'the children are the inspiration'.

Implicit in all of the references to 'relationship' was this sentiment expressed by one of the group: 'through the right kind of relationships that teachers have with people, they will liberate the creativity that their students have'.

'Being in relationship' can, of course, be threatening in some contexts, and/or for some people. One adviser in secondary education said, 'I am not into personal relationships, but that is so important in education.' Reflecting on how he had come into education, he went on to say: 'you don't necessarily go into education for the relationships quality, you go in for the subject element.' He even went on to suggest: 'that's one of the reasons why we hit all the problems in secondary education.' The teacher who enters the profession with little regard for the relationships is, I would suggest, rarer in the primary sector, but nevertheless the intensity of relationships is not one which all individuals find easy, or relish.

However, the overall emphasis on 'relationship' in our research group does reflect the focus and findings of much literature researching primary teachers' work (Woods, 1990, 1995; Woods and Jeffrey, 1996; Cooper and McIntyre, 1996a, 1996b). The importance of 'relationship' to learners is also well documented, both in terms of relationships between learners and in their relationships with educators (Cullingford, 1991; Delamont and Galton, 1987; Jackson, 1987; Pollard, 1987; Sluckin, 1987).

Knowing what you need for yourself, in order to function happily and willingly as a part of dynamic relationships with colleagues and pupils, is vital. The practical strategies suggested in Chapter 9, building on this chapter as a foundation, may help you to identify your own needs.

Summing up so far

Drawing on my recent research project I have suggested that:

- one of the biggest challenges for teachers is knowing and nourishing oneself, and that

- choosing the creative path as an educator and in wider life may be viewed as dispositional and not a matter of ability.

I went on to explore aspects of nurturing self esteem, in order to foster professional artistry.

In the final part of this chapter I look at some issues involved in culture and creativity.

Creativity in cultural context

Elsewhere, I have argued that creativity, like all constructs, is an embedded term (Craft *et al.*, 1997). By this I mean that the meaning and scope, manifestation and relevance of creativity are all subject to cultural context. For example, some of my earlier research work took place with teachers of English in primary schools in southern Spain. During one of my visits there, a primary teacher commented to me that he felt creativity had nothing to do with education. In the discussion which ensued, we established that, from his perspective, in Spain teachers and schools are seen as conveying knowledge and skills but not an approach to life which is about creativity. This is a view held by other teachers with whom I have worked, in both England and Spain. And yet, I have witnessed teachers in both countries facilitating and inspiring creativity in their pupils. But what my work in Spain has made me much more conscious of is how the surrounding culture affects the ways in which teachers do it. One of the research instruments in that particular study was a teacher-attitude survey, through which we discovered in our sample a very low value given to the fostering of creativity in schools (Craft, Pain and Shepherd, 1996).

It is important, then, to acknowledge the place within society of creativity – and also of teachers. In Spain, all teachers are civil servants, with permanent posts. Teachers are viewed as authority figures within the community and accorded respect by pupils and parents. Schools are considered to be places of professional expertise. Deference is shown toward the teacher's professional judgement – even when, as was the case with one teacher observed, the teacher in fact knows little about the subject being taught (this particular individual had been allocated the teaching of English because he had studied French as an undergraduate, and was the only member of staff who had studied languages to degree level; however, he was unable to hold a conversation in English and took advantage of having two English speaking visitors in his classroom to learn from native speakers himself, alongside his class).

Consequently teachers in Spain have a strong sense of professional purpose and to a degree consider themselves expert in their domain. As discussed earlier, if this is undermined it is done so from within the education system (through teachers' perceptions of the reforms in education), rather than from outside.

However, during informal discussions with students and with the research team, few of the teachers in this sample considered creativity to be particularly relevant to society. This pattern of values may reflect the economic and social context in Spain, where the impact of the accelerating pace of global techno-logical and social change is not yet felt in any real way. It may also reflect the stability felt by teachers as authority figures embedded in their communities.

The lack of importance accorded to creativity in education has been documented elsewhere. From her research with teachers across the UK, Fryer (1996) describes how only 17 per cent of teachers in the Collings and Fryer survey (1991) were really positive about creativity.

It seems likely, however, as argued by others (Hegelson, 1990; Glasser, 1992), that the pace of global change will demand an increasing emphasis on fostering pupil creativity. I would suggest that this will involve using pedagogy, which involves both person centredness and intentional strategies, in such a way that the pedagogy fits appropriately with the culture of which it is a part. So, pedagogical styles which are appropriate in southern Spain may not be so in Madrid, or in London, or Glasgow, or Llandrindod Wells. And this also means that what counts as pupil creativity is influenced by the cultural and domain context.

A Spanish case study

For this study, involving twenty-eight teachers in a small rural town in south-west Spain, our research observations were almost exclusively of whole-class teaching. This in part reflects the dominant local practice. We observed a number of general pedagogical features and classified these for analysis using Alexander's (1996) categories of analysis for whole-class teaching in cross-cultural settings: organisation, discourse and values.

Organisationally, the whole class was almost exclusively taught en bloc, with the exception of some pair role play in one class, which nevertheless involved the rest of the class watching. There was a level of informality in each of the classes observed, although the teacher remained in charge, usually standing up, mainly at the front of the room, occasionally moving through the rows of children to the other end of the room. In each of the classes observed, the teacher's desk faced the children, and the board formed a focal point on which the teacher wrote frequently during the lesson to illustrate spelling and grammar. Differentiation for children achieving highly or struggling with the lesson content was provided purely in terms of the level of spoken interaction with the pupils.

The *discourse* revolved around use of the text book, which in common with local practice all teachers observed relied heavily upon (one scheme only; no 'pick and mixing'). Each child had a text book open on the desk throughout each lesson even when this was minimally referred to. The lessons observed involved a great deal of speaking and listening, as might be expected in lessons focusing on learning a new language. The verbal work was reinforced in some cases by the limited wall displays (most classrooms had nothing at all on the walls, and where there were displays they did not include children's (or teachers') work, but rather printed matter, commercial posters and so on). Concepts were taught 'by the book', teachers frequently referring to the manual during the lesson. Understanding was checked by repetition, questioning and through role play exercises dictated by the text book. Pupils appeared motivated even though the content of the learning was not personalised for them. Many children were proud of their language skills and wished to practise with English-speaking visitors at the beginning and end of lessons.

Values conveyed by the teachers observed included expectations about behaviour (an understanding that the teacher was in charge) and focus (the learning of each child was the focus). Each child was valued, whilst knowledge was manifestly held and passed on by the teacher as expert, backed up by the text book. In the lessons we observed, achievement was defined against the text book criteria of being able to speak, listen, understand and translate key phrases, in an orderly way, following the teacher's guidance.

Strategies which appeared to foster learner creativity

Learner creativity in this context meant pupils being able to make connections of their own, to come up with new combinations, to apply imagination to their use of language, to operate as English speakers beyond the particular expectations of the classroom. Strategies which the research team found to be associated with particularly effective fostering of such pupil creativity included:

- use of humour (one teacher used many different techniques within one lesson to get his class laughing, from mixed-up words such as 'dalsa' for salad, 'rtacos' for carrots, to unusual and amusing combinations, such as 'spider steak');
- friendly coaxing of individuals;
- calling on individuals by name;
- generally high teacher expectations including positive insistence on getting the answers right (for most pupils – not for those who were struggling); and
- keeping the pace fast.

In such classrooms there was an atmosphere of excitement, of ease and of inclusion. Each child was treated as both a member of the class as a whole, and also an individual in their own right.

Learner creativity in this context meant pupils being able to make connections of their own, to come up with new combinations, to apply imagination to their use of language, to operate as English speakers beyond the particular expectations of the classroom.

Other characteristics of successful teachers' pedagogy were firm control and authentic teacher–pupil relationships.

FIRM CONTROL (TEACHER-CENTRED BUT LEARNER-FOCUSED)

Control was held in different styles by each individual. In part clearly it came from pupils' expectations; all of the teachers observed were held in high esteem – in turn partly a cultural characteristic where the teacher was seen as the source of knowledge and embodiment of authority. Strategies for holding firm control in a teacher-centred but learner-focused manner included having clear ground rules on classroom management (in general the pupils were all seated, the teacher standing; in general the arrangement of the room meant that pupils and teachers were facing one another, and could easily make eye contact).

Throughout lessons where the teacher was successfully fostering pupil creativity, the teacher remained the centre of control. But at the heart of this was the learner, thus these lessons were 'learner-focused'. Also implied in this term is the powerful use of relationship with individual pupils, discussed next.

AUTHENTIC TEACHER–PUPIL RELATIONSHIPS

Pupils were made to feel that their teacher knew they were there, and that they, personally, mattered. Relationships were authentic; there was a great deal of warmth between teachers and pupils, and a sense in which teachers knew the children's context (for example, their locality), if not the details of their lives. The children's home context was a part of the lessons. During one spoken exercise about explaining where they lived, for example, the teacher demonstrated that she knew exactly where each child lived. Consequently pupils were constantly alert for personal contact, focused on their classroom performance.

These strategies mirror the findings of others. The playfulness involved in using humour is documented by Gardner (1993) and also Shagoury Hubbard (1996) as a critical part of fostering creativity.

Fryer (1994), whose work was cited at the start of this chapter, found moderate to high correlation between orientation to creativity and 'person orientation', or the valuing of relationships. She notes that the most creative teachers succeed in actively and deeply engaging each pupil in learning and thinking for themselves. They also echo the recommendations of Shagoury Hubbard (1996) whose writing is based on ethnographic field work in Alaskan primary classrooms. Shagoury Hubbard talks about pupil creativity being fostered in an environment which has both structure and freedom; flexible predictability, where pupils are respected as capable thinkers, where expectations are high, and where relationships between adults and children are authentic.

These links with existing research based in other cultures may be an indication that there may be some features of pedagogy which fosters creativity which transcend culture. However, it seems to me that there may be some features of the pedagogy which we observed which were culture-specific; these may include classroom organisation and the values attached by pupils and teachers alike to the teacher role.

Summary of Chapter 7

Earlier in the chapter I explored some of the challenges involved in knowing and nourishing oneself as a teacher and put forward the idea that being creative is dispositional rather than based on ability. I also explored aspects of nurturing one's self-esteem as a teacher as a foundation to enabling professional artistry.

In the latter part of the chapter I looked at aspects of the cultural embeddedness of creativity, drawing for illustration on some of my research work in southern Spain.

Acknowledgements

I would like to thank all of the educators with whom I have worked in England and in Spain, and whose practice has informed this chapter. Also Tom Lyons, my co-researcher on the London project, Jana Dugal and Christine Kimberley at the former Institute for Creativity in London, Toni Pain at the University of Extremadura in Caceres, Spain and Rick Shepherd, formerly with Oxford University Press in Madrid, with whom so much of my thinking and research on creativity has developed. Finally, thanks are also due to our colleagues in the Centre for Curriculum and Teaching Studies at The Open University, who have awarded grants to support some of the research cited here.

Note

1 Details of the project and its background can be found in a seminar paper (Craft and Lyons, 1996) available from Anna Craft at The Open University, also in two journal papers (Craft, 1996b and 1997), and in an article written for *The Times Educational Supplement* by Jonathan Croall (1996).

8 Fostering creativity in the primary classroom

In this chapter I explore some of the conditions for and characteristics of creative teaching and learning.

Space in which to create

Fostering creativity requires commitment to space: physical and conceptual. Creating space means being conscious of the physical place of your classroom, and ways in which it may foster children's creativity. It is important to consider not simply the layout of physical space but also the resourcing of any activity and of the learning environment. If children are to be encouraged to think independently in any area of the curriculum, they will need easy access to materials including books, the computer/s, atlases, games, construction materials, puzzles, craft materials and so on. They will need to be able at times to work with others, in pairs and in groups, so the classroom space needs to support all of these possibilities.

Classrooms which foster creativity also operate in a special way conceptually. They allow mistakes and encourage experimentation, openness and risk-taking. Shallcross (1981) argues that it is important for each child to have sufficient physical space and time in any learning activity, in order to do just this. And this includes our own interventions in children's thinking. As she says: 'Too often we have a tendency to intervene earlier than we should while a student is working something out ... Those early interventions often discourage rather than encourage' (p. 15). One of the most important lessons I have learned as a teacher was that offered to me when I was still training to become a primary teacher, by Wendla Kernig, who was at that time the head of Eveline Lowe Primary School in South London. She spoke of listening to and watching children to ascertain what kinds of teacher interventions might be appropriate. Observation, noticing what individual children themselves are noticing, interested by, focusing on, enables us as educators to make appropriate interventions, and at the appropriate moment.

Giving children space and watching what they are noticing is not, however, to say that structure and content are unimportant. Clear expectations around the nature of learning opportunities are important. I would support the view put forward by the Plowden Committee, which advocated child-centred learning approaches, that although 'the sense of personal discovery influences the intensity of a child's experience, the vividness of his memory and the probability of effective transfer of learning . . . At the same time it is true that trivial ideas and methods may be 'discovered' . . . furthermore, time does not allow children to find their way by discovery to all they have to learn' (CACE, 1967). Dominant learning theories such as Vygotskian social constructivism rather emphasise the importance of 'modelling' and 'scaffolding' children's understandings from what they know to what they do not. I also accept the principle behind the introduction of a national curriculum in England and Wales, which seeks to offer equality of opportunity to all children. What I am suggesting is that space for conversation, interactions which actually seek the child's perspective, is important in fostering children's creativity.

Consider this case study from a classroom of 9 and 10 year olds in North London.

The children were invited to participate in a 'passion assembly' – in other words, to create something to represent what they are passionate about. Sabine wrote a 2,000 word story about cruelty to animals. It was really a short novel. An identifiable achievement, it was rightly praised and validated by her teacher and by the head teacher in the school. But Jason's passion was for cooking. His pride in his achievement in creating and icing a sponge cake in the shape of his favourite food, pasta, was not given the same recognition and esteem as his friend's story. Why not?

The case study illustrates that educating for creativity must involve acknowledging all of the different ways in which children are able to exercise possibility thinking; thinking back to the conceptual framework of people, processes and domains, it is important to recognise the domains in which children enjoy expressing themselves/exploring. It means, too, acknowledging different personal styles of creating.

Making space for creativity, then, means valuing it, in as many different ways as children may express it. It means creating an overt 'mental climate' as Shallcross (1981) calls it. It includes fostering self-worth and self-esteem. The creative teacher values both achievability and relevance of classroom activities for the children. Achievability means setting challenges for the children which are achievable, to build confidence. Earlier writers such as McClelland (cited in Rosen *et al.*, 1969) referred to this as 'achievement motivation'. Relevance means checking out children's perspectives on their learning activities, particularly now that the curriculum, even for nursery children, is defined externally and some would say imposed on the teacher–pupil relationship. Woods and Jeffrey (1996) in their study of creativity in primary classrooms describe how the teachers negotiate knowledge which is relevant and meaningful to the children, attempting to negotiate the gap between the public knowledge of the National Curriculum and the personal knowledge of each child.

Creative teaching as good teaching

I would argue, as others have done, that creative teaching is 'good teaching'. Quite simply, teaching is a job which requires and involves fostering creativity. Ironically, perhaps, this is acknowledged within official documentation from Teaching As a Career (TASC), which was until recently based in the Department for Education (TASC, 1994a, 1994b) but which is now absorbed within the Teacher Training Agency. Those who have written on creativity in education talk about 'creativity as part of normality, as part of everyday actions and ideas' (Halliwell, 1993: 69). Halliwell describes creativity in teaching as being 'inventive flexibility' because no two groups of learners are identical, and because no two days are the same. Flexibility, she suggests, is underpinned by anticipation and imagination, backed up by strong organisation and judgement (control over ideas). Creative teaching is, she suggests, consciously monitored. It depends then, on the following qualities:

- a clear sense of need;
- the ability to read a situation;
- the willingness to take risks;
- the ability to monitor and evaluate events.

(Halliwell, 1993: 71)

The notion of having volition is also embedded in Woods' (1990) description of creative teaching as involving ownership, control, relevance and innovation (for both teacher and learner). Interpreting Woods' criteria, Jeffrey has suggested the following (1997): 'This may involve in any given situation some or all of these features, an innovative idea or approach, some ownership and control over the process by the teacher and the pupil, and the event must be relevant to both teacher and pupil.' For me, one of the most significant elements in the work of Woods and Jeffrey is the range of individual voices and perspectives – including those of children.

What children can tell us

In a recent in-depth study of children's own attitudes toward being in creative environments involving 140 children in five classrooms, Jeffrey and Woods (1997) discovered four aspects of classroom experience where the children whom they interviewed particularly appreciated the efforts of their teachers in respect of:

- responding to children's feelings (including acknowledging the range of the feelings, and also helping children to feel confident);
- engaging the children's interest (including having a sense of humour, making the learning fun, having imaginative ideas and a resourceful approach);
- maintaining the children's own autonomy/identity (including giving space

to children to develop and implement their own ideas – to think for themselves, including being heard during discussions and disputes, and also allowing children to adopt their own preferred styles of working);

• encouraging children's capacity to reflect critically (through encouraging rational analysis, even when it could include criticism of the teacher, and also by role-detachment between 'their total involvement and the ability to reflect and comment upon their involvement'.

(Jeffrey and Woods, 1997: 31)

The Jeffrey and Woods study draws attention to the need for trust in a creative classroom. The emotional climate of the classroom needs to offer each child personal confidence and security; as Shallcross writes, 'the ground rules are personal guarantees that allow [children] to grow at their own rate, retain the privacy of their work until they are ready to share it, and prize their possible differences' (1981: 19).

Children can also tell us what they need in order to create. They do this both explicitly and implicitly. Sabine needed time, silence and a feeling of security in order to write. Jason, too, needed time, and he liked also to have the radio or music playing, a range of cooking facilities and ingredients and to feel trusted. They could each articulate explicitly some of their needs, and others could be observed by watching them. Sabine was more fortunate than Jason in school in that her teacher had noticed that she needed long periods of time for her writing, and structured the class creative writing mornings each week so that children who needed longer could have sustained concentration on their work, whereas those who finished earlier could go on to other activities.

'Hearing' what children are telling us they need to enable them to learn and create effectively is an important aspect of the artistry of teaching.

In the next part of this chapter I want to look at some of the characteristics of fostering creativity in the classroom, starting with the teacher's perspective and going on to look at ways in which creativity is an expression of holism, in the sense of manifesting both the conscious and the non-conscious.

Teachers and the creating mind

What do teachers make of the creating mind?

In a study of over 1,000 teachers' attitudes toward creativity, Fryer and Collings (1991) found that most teachers in the study saw creativity in terms of 'imagination', 'originality' and 'self-expression'. Only half regarded 'divergence' as relevant to creativity. Convergent thinking was only seen as relevant by 10.2 per cent of the sample – presumably because very few teachers in the study saw 'possibility thinking' as a core process to creativity. Few teachers saw creativity as involving mysterious processes (9.1 per cent). Rather more thought unconscious processes were involved (18.1 per cent). About half saw creativity as involving inspiration (46.6 per cent).

As far as pedagogy is concerned, Fryer and Collings found that teachers highly orientated to creativity had a preference for a pupil-orientated approach to teaching (a finding in my own research with Spanish primary teachers: Craft, Pain and Shepherd, 1996). Fryer and Collings identify an underlying value system linked to 'person orientation', particularly for women teachers and for those specialising in the humanities.

Creativity in the classroom – the conscious and the non-conscious

Within the many conceptions of mind – philosophical, psychological, socio-logical, anthropological, religious – a common basic distinction is one between the conscious mind and the non-conscious. Whatever explanation framework we put around them, the distinction remains that human beings who are beyond a certain age in childhood experience some aspects of mind with awareness, i.e. with consciousness, and, by contrast, other aspects without. Within the curriculum, pedagogy and assessment of our schools, we tend to place higher value on the conscious aspect of mind than on the non-conscious, as touched on earlier in the book. Yet, there is plenty of evidence that both the conscious and the non-conscious play a role in creativity.

The aspect of the conscious which I want to emphasise in the development of creativity is 'insight' – the ability to build sense-making bridges between different experiences and stimuli, and to be able to reflect on these. I would suggest that insight both encompasses and is larger than the intellect. For although the *sources* of insight may not be at all conscious or rational, often logic can be imposed upon insightful moments, after the event. For example, a teacher planning her classroom at the start of a new school year may find herself moving furniture about through 'feel' and it is only once the move has been orchestrated that she can explain the learning logic behind the new arrangement.

There are those (Perkins, 1995, 1997) who would claim that insight involves logic even if we are unaware of it. Insight is something which we can attempt to get better at, as Sternberg and Lubart (1995) have suggested. I would suggest that developing one's insight involves disposition and skill, and encompasses both inspiration and action. In this sense the development of insight is equatable to Kenny's creative imagination (Kenny, 1989). It is distinct from 'fancy' (which, as Coleridge (1954) suggests, merely reproduces what is); Kenny suggests (p. 114) that imagination is 'superior to the intellect'.

The non-conscious aspect of mind, on the other hand, encompasses dreams, daydreams and other aspects of the unconscious which remain at least in part hidden to us. What those who have written about the non-conscious suggest, however, is that the role of the non-conscious should not be underestimated in facilitating insight. Theoretical characterisations include a whole spectrum of approaches which include computational models (Boden, 1992; West, 1991), creative cognition (Ward, Finke and Smith, 1995), logical/behaviour based (Perkins, 1995, 1997; Claxton, 1997), psychoanalytic/psychosynthetic based on Freudian and Jungian ideas (Adams, 1986; Assagioli, 1974; Winnicott, 1971;

Ross, 1978), neurological (Zdenek, 1985), affective-sensory (Edwards, 1990) and so on.

Harnessing and stimulating creativity in the classroom needs then to involve and value the non-conscious as well as the conscious. In the example given above, of the teacher organising the room for the start of the school year by drawing on the 'feel' for how it could be laid out, there may be gatekeepers other than herself who have a claim on the way the room 'should' be organised. These gatekeepers may include the head or senior colleagues, other teaching staff, the school keeper, even the cleaner. Their claims may cut across a teacher's effectiveness in following her unarticulated insight into how the room could be set out. Thus her creativity as a teacher could be thwarted, despite the fact that she is a relatively powerful and experienced creator in this regard. Consider then, how much greater the chances of a school unwittingly blocking the non-conscious creative insights of children, given their relative powerlessness in claims on time, space, knowledge and experience.

The body and feelings as elements in fostering creativity

I would argue that other aspects of the whole person play roles, too, in fostering creativity: body and feelings being two of these.

Body, or the physical, is an element in our experience of the world, in at least two ways: first, as in the case of the birth of a child, it provides a biological 'engine' of action; second, we may have physical responses to our experiences. Thus, as Edwards has argued, in the processes of teaching and learning, the body is trained in specific ways, and we learn what is appropriate to express and experience through our physical selves in that environment (Edwards, 1997). McWilliam, writing from a feminist perspective, suggests that we underestimate the importance of the ways in which teachers express their passion for knowledge through their bodies. Thus the teacher provides the 'biological engine' in learning – McWilliam argues that legitimising the place of the teacher's body in the learning process may result in 'powerful pedagogy of a most elating and transformative kind' (McWilliam, 1996). I would suggest that the learner experiences the classroom or learning environment on a physical, as well as intellectual, spiritual and emotional level.

Some approaches explicitly value this, naming learning through the body 'visceral' learning (Institute for Creativity, 1995), although traditionally in schools we tend not to acknowledge the body in learning, except insofar as it is necessary for the knowledge or skill being acquired.

It seems to me that, in a similar way to the body, feelings are both a form of experiencing and a vehicle for expressing. The deep-seatedness of feelings in meaning-making has been highlighted by Goleman's work (1996). And as many have suggested (Holt, 1992; Pintrich, Marx and Boyle, 1993; Jeffrey and Woods, 1997) the way in which a learner feels may have a huge impact on what is learned, and how, and what is later associated with that learning experience.

Feelings, the teacher, teaching and learning

Teachers have a critical role in shaping a vision for educating which responds with compassion to growing uncertainty and instability. In addition to the literature about the learner and feelings, there is growing interest in exploring the nature of the educator's emotional experience of their work (Nias, 1996), and the overlap of personal with professional identity (la Porte, 1996; Little, 1996; McWilliam, 1996; Revell, 1996; Woods and Jeffrey, 1996). Some of the reasons for the deeply affective dimension of teaching are drawn out by Nias, who suggests, first, the intensity of personal interactions involved in the process of teaching and, second, that for many teachers their personal identity is closely merged with their professional one, so that self-esteem is closely tied to the classroom or school. Finally she suggests that teachers feel so strongly about their work *because* they invest so heavily in it (Nias, 1996).

What I am highlighting, then, is the emotional reality of the job of teaching, which necessarily provides a part of the context for learning in education institutions.

I want to look now at some aspects of spirit, linking these with the non-conscious aspect of mind.

A spiritual dimension to fostering creativity

As discussed in Chapter 2, in my formulation of the non-conscious I have found it useful to draw on Assagioli's (1974) psychosynthetic theory of the divided self, itself drawn from Freudian and Jungian ideas. I suggest that the intuitive, impulsive self, which may be the source of inspiration and generative action (and thus of possibility thinking), is non-conscious, unlike the transcendent, conscious, rational self (which Assagioli calls the 'I'), which drinks from and is nourished by, among other places, the non-conscious self.

One aspect of western culture is the esteem in which we hold the rational and the conscious (and rational), above the non-conscious and the intuitive (and perhaps above the physical). Thus when we talk, for example, of teachers undergoing continuing professional development or children studying history, it is perhaps unusual to assume that these will involve meditation, intuition or locating a feeling in the body.

I would question how appropriate it is to divorce 'mystery' or spirit and feelings of connection with the wider universe ('spiritual' for short) from rationality/ intellectuality. I propose that the non-conscious and the spiritual may be conceived of as being intertwined. This may be close to Gardner's proposed existential intelligence (Gardner, 1996).

In making this proposal I draw on the writing of Bohm and Peat, two scientists who suggest that scientific creativity is inhibited by over-dependence on the conscious, the rational and the rule-bound (Bohm and Peat, 1989). This is not to say that creative expression does not involve any of these things, indeed they suggest (and others have also argued) that 'to live in a creative way requires extreme and sensitive perception of the orders and structures of relationship to individuals, society and nature' (Bohm and Peat, 1989: 231). But they suggest that we need to acknowledge and value intuitive ways of knowing, to draw on what they call the 'implicate order'.

They suggest that our implicate understandings are often far more complex than our explicate ones, and they can be difficult to articulate. What is significant about implicate ideas is their generative potential. In other words, the flash of understanding which is so hard to explain, holds within it many possible unfoldments. They suggest we need more access to the implicate orders which underlie our explicate ones, because they are the source of generative ideas, in other words, of our creativity.

They argue that we need a new kind of 'creative surge' at the end of the twentieth century, which will enable us to find ways of breaking out of rigidity. I would argue, with Bohm and Peat, that we now need to foster an order of creativity which extends into social organisation, science, culture and consciousness. What this may mean is giving voice to our implicate and generative selves. I would like to suggest that that is where our creative intelligence lies.

Bohm and Peat's conception of the implicate seems, then, to include the non-conscious (and intuitive) with the spiritual – in the sense of connection with the wider universe. In adopting their position I, too, conflate the two notions.

The notion of the implicate may provide an explanation for, and may foster, insights which appear to come in a flash. It has something in common with the writing of Perkins, Jay and Tishman. In their discussion of the long search process which precedes apparent 'flashes' of insight, they argue that human cognition appears well-adapted to the search which is almost all non-conscious. They also suggest that modern theories of evolution imply order and insightfulness in the behaviour of genetic material over long periods of time (Perkins, Jay and Tishman, 1993). The implicate order may, then, have insight or intelligence.

I will return to this notion of the implicate order in Chapter 11. For now, I simply want to flag that fostering creativity in the classroom may involve acknowledging one's own non-conscious spiritual connections with the wider universe, as well as those of children.

In the last part of this chapter I want to look at what might need to be done to increase the value placed on creativity in the classroom.

A discourse for describing creativity in the classroom

It has been argued (Jeffrey, 1997) that the current emphasis on achieving uniformity in teaching performance, evaluated through inspection, itself involving much bureaucracy, has had a variety of effects on teachers' practice. One of these has been the undermining of a professional language for investigating and describing practice. Jeffrey has suggested that

> perhaps teachers do not credit their own creative acts because much of it goes unrecorded and therefore unrecognised. In spite of teachers regretting

the diminution of spontaneity in terms of curriculum organisation (Pollard *et al.* 1994 pp. 85) there are still many spontaneous acts relating to specific activities in teachers' classrooms. Much of this action, because of its sponta-neous nature, is unrecorded and therefore does not achieve status in a discourse (like that of OFSTED) which is trying to establish uniformity.

(Jeffrey and Woods, 1998)

It seems timely to make a shift toward what Jeffrey calls 'the appreciation of creative teaching', despite the fact that teaching is often viewed by teachers as a role which requires and involves fostering creativity. As indicated above, Fryer and Collings (1991) found that very few teachers regard themselves as particularly creative, 'the most frequently selected attributes tended to be concerned with social attributes and willingness to work hard' (p. 211). Jeffrey's explanation for this is the lack of opportunity which teachers have to identify and value their own creativity or to observe it in the practice of others.

Appreciating creative teaching involves developing a discourse of both language and behaviour. Jeffrey (1997) suggests a range of collaborative and collegial strategies which may foster such appreciation of classroom artistry, including reciprocal shadowing, reflecting back, reflecting on and analysing classroom practice. Drawing on his own experience as a collaborative researcher of creative classroom practice suggests that the discussion stemming from these strategies may involve:

- asking questions;
- offering analysis;
- making assertions; and
- being controversial.

From his own research he suggests a range of 'frames' for interpreting or 'viewing' the creative practice of a particular teacher with whom he worked. These are:

- inspired actions;
- generation of atmospheres;
- knowledge engagement; and
- negotiative approaches.

I would like to suggest that valuing one's own practice enough to investigate it in the way in which Jeffrey suggests involves an act of bravery. The primary classroom often represents a manifestation of teacher values, some held unconsciously. Investigating one's professional practices may involve laying these bare and can, as Dadds (1995) has argued, be deeply challenging at a personal level.

Building on Jeffrey's term, I want to suggest ways in which we as teachers need to re-frame our practice in order to enable creativity. I explore this issue in Chapter 9.

As part of the discourse which focuses reframing our practice, I want to emphasise the need for a more fully developed language to describe the creativity of children. How, for example, do we distinguish clearly between a child's creative play as opposed to play which is purely mimicry? How do we draw a more clear cut distinction in language between a learning environment which is fostering creativity as opposed to fantasy?

Summing up

In this chapter I have explored some possible conditions for fostering creativity in the classroom. I have suggested that these include:

- making space conceptually and physically;
- 'good teaching' – which involves a feel for appropriateness to individual learners, backed up by imagination and flexibility, as well as conscious monitoring of practice;
- listening to what children tell us.

In exploring characteristics of creativity in the classroom I have explored:

- the role of non-conscious routes to insight, as well as the conscious;
- the idea that creativity is fostered through holistic engagement between teachers, learners and domains, involving mind, body, feelings and spirit.

Finally, I discussed the need for practitioners to develop a discourse for describing creativity in education, at the level of their own practice and more widely in the teaching profession.

9 Professional development for creativity

In this chapter, I discuss some of the implications for professional development, of reframing practice. I look at the form and content of continuing professional development (CPD) which might be appropriate, and also explore some of the barriers to such CPD which may be encountered by teachers and schools. The chapter builds on the two preceding it and provides a foundation for the final part of the book.

In this chapter I draw on the study of educators in south-east England which I introduced in Chapter 7 and also the notion of 'framing' professional practice, introduced in Chapter 8, in order to explore practical strategies for professional development in order to foster creativity in learners.

Reframing practice

In Chapter 8, I discussed Jeffrey's (1997) concept of the frame through which to view one's practice. A frame provides both a descriptive snapshot and also a set of values which can be used to analyse what is seen. A frame is therefore an interpretive tool – and will also affect what we choose to notice. As Jeffrey puts it: 'in observing a teacher's practice for creative events, the observer must decide what he or she will be sensitive to' (p. 60) and, clearly, there is artistry involved in the selection of what is appropriate, as Jeffrey argues: 'Observation of creative practices is an appreciation of qualities, those aspects of the practice that are germane to the situation' (p. 60). Thus, he suggests, observing practice is a little like becoming a connoisseur of wine; through observation, one develops 'frames' through which to appreciate and analyse the teacher's work. As part of reframing, I would suggest, one develops a language for describing and analysing what is observed, which itself feeds back into and enriches the practice under investigation.

I want to suggest that giving the fostering of creativity a higher priority in the classroom may mean reframing practice at the level of the individual as well as the collective (school, LEA, education system). This chapter is addressed at the level of the individual teacher, developing and reframing practice.

I would argue that the fostering of creativity in others involves, at the least, awareness of one's teaching strategies and, in a much broader sense, a familiarity with the frameworks which we create as educators – for ourselves as well as for the learners in our care. Much of this next part of the chapter involves nurturing one's own self-esteem as a teacher and draws on the research project introduced in Chapter 7. Later in the chapter I go on to look at relationships in the school and its community, and barriers to fostering creativity which may be encountered.

Risk and teacher identity

A useful question to ask yourself is the one often asked by Jana Dugal, former Director of the Institute for Creativity: 'Am I what I teach?' Most teachers have a very strong identity as a teacher, particularly those teaching 3–11 year olds. However, do you allow yourself to be swallowed up by teaching and what you teach? In Chapter 7, I cited evidence that teachers of young children often see themselves as providers for children, perhaps to the exclusion of their own needs at times. Asking yourself the question 'Am I what I teach?' on a regular basis is a way of starting to identify what you need in order to be 'you'. And being more aware of the nourishment which you need for yourself is a critical part of being able to foster creativity in others.

The commitment to 'risk' – another strong theme in the research project (Craft, 1996b and 1997) – provides another practical challenge. 'Risk' implies a broaching of boundaries, the 'going beyond', the breaking with convention described by Gardner (1993b). Examples from our project included a youth worker deciding to create a workshop on a cappella (unaccompanied) singing for young women only, where they could compose and perform songs from the heart. This resulted in discovering that one child was being abused; it also resulted in another child gaining enough confidence to go for a recording contract with a record label, which she achieved. In this particular case it also ultimately led to the youth worker in question taking the risk of becoming a singer herself, and making her very first CD, containing songs she had composed, arranged and performed herself. An example from within the school setting was a teacher of 6 and 7 year olds adapting his plans at the drop of a hat to take his class outside into the snow even though it was not encouraged within the school, and it seems likely, as Hargreaves has predicted (1994), that we will see an increasing recognition by educators of the need to take risks, for themselves and for learners with whom they work.

Finding out what you need is a process which can bring with it surprises. It can also mean taking some risks – risking hearing things which you didn't know you were seeking, and which you may not know how to accommodate. It is guaranteed to bring change and development.

Openness and receptivity

A theme which arose from the research project was the belief among the educator group that creativity involves 'receptivity' or 'openness' to a wide range of influences, including those which are spiritual and intuitive. This belief echoes points made by Fritz (1943) about having vision and then allowing ideas to 'germinate' and 'assimilate', and by Gardner (1993a) about valuing creativity across the different intelligences. It also appears to be parallel with the writing of Csikszentmihalyi (1994) in which he reports that artists with whom he worked demonstrated openness to experiences and impulses, and echoes Gardner's (1993b) discussion of great creators.

Personal nourishment, it seems to me, involves the same quality of openness or receptivity. One educator in the project awoke in the middle of the night feeling a burning sensation in her mind and body. She found herself first writing it as a poem and then painting it. Eventually this process provided the focus for a workshop which she offered at a national conference. It is similar to the experience reported earlier in Chapter 2, of the educator who awoke in the night hearing music playing, and who played it out on the piano, eventually making it into a learning experience in her educator role. The act of being open both nourished the unconscious self, and was integral to both of these educators' roles in fostering creativity with learners. Another teacher described how at the time in his life when he got married, he was somehow able to be receptive to lots of impulses and ideas which in his conscious mind he didn't know were there – leading to a huge class-based project with the infant children he was teaching. The act of being open, which originated in his personal life, nourished his non-conscious self in enabling a new idea to grow and be implemented in school. And a teacher of drama described great enjoyment in expressing her own feelings to her students, and vice versa.

Thus, an aspect of professional development is seeking ways of encouraging receptivity and openness in oneself.

Offering the non-conscious a voice

The notion of being inseparable in identity from one's role as a teacher is a common one as already discussed. One of the primary teachers in our project told us 'I don't think you can separate yourself and your teaching.' A powerful part of yourself is your non-conscious mind, the source of impulses, sensations and feelings, which is often non-logical, and thus a part of yourself which is bound up in your role is the non-conscious. When I talk about nourishing the unconscious, I am referring to Assagioli's (1974) distinction, introduced in Chapter 2, between the 'I' and 'self', the former referring to sensation, emotion/feeling, impulse/desire, imagination, thought, intuition and will. The 'I' refers to the conscious self which has the capacity to transcend, or disidentify from, the 'self'.

What follows are five practical strategies for reframing the role of the non-conscious in practice. The aim is to offer the non-conscious more of a voice in triggering one's own creativity and in being aware of possibilities in fostering it in learners. The strategies are as follows: reflections; finding space; dreams and daydreams; imaging/visualisation; and, finally, concretising images. They are all drawn from the research project.

Reflections

In our project we noted the tendency in educators to value aspects of creative teaching which they themselves want/need. Descriptions of 'mirroring' in this way are widespread in personal growth literature (Edwards, 1993). In the psychoanalytic tradition, the concept is named 'projection' – Freud first described it as a 'defensive mechanism' operating in the cases of hysteria which he was studying (1894). Later, he called the same defence mechanism 'repression', and later still his daughter Anna Freud (1936) listed projection as just one of twelve aspects of repression. The idea was later developed by Melanie Klein (Segal, 1964; Ogden, 1982). The idea in projection is that sometimes people feel and behave as though important aspects of their own selves are contained in others.

Ways of 'turning the mirror around', in order to learn from the reflection include:

- Noticing how you organise your life at present: everything which you do serves some kind of a purpose for you, even if it feels as though some are not that helpful. Some of your current way of living already nourishes you as a creative educator; other aspects undermine it. Notice which does which.
- Notice what you tend to have strong reactions to in your life. There may be situations or people who really make you frustrated, and others which or whom you adore. Often we are more aware of what annoys us than what makes us happy. What annoys us is often a reflection of something within ourselves which we dislike, or which needs attention.

As part of the creativity in education course which formed part of the research project was a weekend workshop, entitled *The Mastery*, taught at the Institute for Creativity. Focused on creating and performing in front of an audience, and giving and receiving feedback, it was in many ways structured around the process of looking at one's own reflection. Many teachers in our project commented on the depth and power of that experience; phrases which were used included 'magic', 'absolutely mind-blowing', 'changed my life, as they say'. Most echoed the comments that *The Mastery* 'gives you permission to explore roles and facets of yourself', and that 'it made you re-examine [your practice] . . . you know we are all sitting there being stopped by what we think is circumstance but is mostly ourselves, and we ought to get on and do these things really.'

That creativity requires ownership and relevance has been well documented (Woods, 1995; Woods and Jeffrey, 1996). In this section I have been suggesting that 'looking in the mirror', or 'noticing your reflection' enables you to see what resources and activities you already have at your fingertips, and perhaps some of the challenges.

Finding space

The notion of clearing time and space was embedded in the course which our research group participated in. It has also been acknowledged by other researchers, such as Feldman (1994) who has written about the way in which the non-conscious mind synthesises ideas and information in a way which can appear to be coincidental to our conscious selves. He argues that insight comes from listening to messages which our non-conscious selves are sending us – through, for example our dreams and daydreams. Through dreams and daydreams we may get flashes of information about a particular aspect of our lives over and over again during a long period of time. If we are to make use of and act on them, we need to make space and time to listen to them.

Space and time may be as short as ten minutes. Space may be also physical; it may involve being in a quiet place, or walking, or swimming, or being in a place of worship, or lying in the bath, or sitting with a cup of tea, or sitting in front of an open fire, or waiting for a train or bus, or meditating. What is significant is making the space empty and without expectations, but regular, so that you build in the possibility of openness to your non-conscious as a normal part of life. It is just time for you, to re-charge and to hear what your spirit might need as nourishment. Cameron (1995) calls this 'making a date with yourself'. Some people find it useful to write things down, allowing the ideas to flow, rather than censoring any, as in brainstorming, except that what is written may well be prose. This process is sometimes referred to as 'journal writing'. For examples of how this can be done, see Holly (1989).

Clearing a space in this way can provide you with direct nourishment or even inspiration. Or it may simply clear a space for you to be in better contact with yourself.

Dreams and daydreams

As Feldman (1994) has argued, new visions, ideas and projects sometimes come to us in symbolic form. Dreams can be a powerful source of information, and also inspiration. Writing down dreams can shed light on how the non-conscious might need to be nourished. Getting in to the habit of jotting down (notes are enough) what you can remember of your dreams, when awakening or whenever is manageable, is a help in starting to remember and then to make sense of symbolic communication through dreams.

Dreams often hold very simple messages. They can be interpreted in many ways, holding within them the solutions to puzzles we have been wondering about, as well as inspiration and vision. They belong to us; it is just that we are not always in tune with this abundant and often wise part of ourselves. I would argue that it is possible to make sense of one's dreams to some degree without having to study any form of dream analysis (and there are several traditions of thought here).

For example, on the night of my return to work from maternity leave, I had a dream that our home was being burgled. The thieves made themselves known to me and were both male. In the dream I was most concerned to protect the baby and his clothes. The burglars agreed to this. My analysis of this dream is that the burglars symbolised the part of me which belongs to the external world, beyond the home; perhaps the traditionally masculine side of me. The thieves, or external world persona, were potentially taking something from the home just as I was concerned that my return to work would do. The concern in the dream that the burglars should leave my son's clothes intact symbolised, I believe, the waking concern that I have to protect my son's persona and not to detract from who he is by my returning to work. Following this interpretation a little further, I wonder whether the threatened and negotiated-over baby clothes might symbolise a lifestyle, and that the baby in the dream may symbolise the new role which I have taken on in becoming a mother; thus the protecting of the clothes may be a wish to maintain that mothering role as powerfully as I maintain a work role as I make the transition back. To return to the question of creativity, I feel confirmed, having had this dream, in my belief that my ability to foster creativity in others now rests on needing to feel that I am being a good enough mother too.

Dreams, then, may offer signals from the non-conscious, although it is important to acknowledge that some people find dreams more accessible than others.

Imaging/visualisation

As Jung discovered (1995), the symbolic forms of dreams can form a part of waking life too. Visualising, or imaging, are easy-to-use techniques which enable us to draw on the metaphors which our unconscious constructs. Imaging, or visualisation, involves relaxing into a semi-meditative state, and then allowing images to form in your mind's eye. You can image or visualise along a specific theme or question, such as 'relationships' or 'what shall I do for assembly', or 'the impending Ofsted inspection', etc. Since what you conjure up comes from your own unconscious wisdom, you can also ask questions of it.

A classroom teacher who was part of the research project tried visualising when her relationship with the head teacher became rather strained. In her visualisation, the symbol for the head teacher was a bush. It was blocking the path, but she saw that the path was surrounded by rough scrub which although not neatly laid out like the path, was quite easy to walk on. She decided to walk around the bush, without being blocked by it. As she did so, she saw that the bush, although large, was in fact quite spindly. As she walked around it, it seemed less important and powerful than it had previously. She drew on her visualisation in taking the decision to work as closely as she could with the deputy and to distance herself from the head – thus 'going around' her.

Several of the educators in our study visualised themselves as a tree, growing in a nurturing environment, for the duration of the course. They interrogated their visual images to find out what kinds of nourishment would be most appropriate for the tree (i.e. for themselves).

For very practical guidance on how to use visualisation and image work, see Edwards (1993), Gawain (1978) and Glouberman (1989). All three offer different ways of inviting and then working with images.

Concretising images

The therapeutic traditions have a long history in making concrete the unconscious. Try sculpting, painting, drawing, playing, writing or even acting out your images. Making your images concrete, in a similar way to brainstorming, can enable the non-conscious to come to visibility and awareness as well as being fun.

Being seen

This chapter has so far been about aspects of professional and personal development which may be important in fostering your own creativity in enabling that of others. The emphasis in this first part of the chapter has been on 'being seen', initially by yourself. It has been based on the principle that the non-conscious can offer access to all kinds of inspiration, and often indicates to us what the next steps in any project may be. I have suggested that knowing yourself includes having some access to your non-conscious mind. The practical suggestions on how to develop your access to your unconscious are based on the idea of 'composting', or 'mulching'. It isn't that the notes of last night's dream will get translated directly into story time with your reception class, just as one rotten apple in your compost heap won't translate instantly into new fertiliser for the rose bush. But allowing your unconscious out in many different ways will, over time, combine to provide a rich ground for inspirations and choices to take root and grow.

In the next section of the chapter I go on to look at forms of professional development which may be appropriate to fostering creativity.

Professional development: forms and foci

It should follow from the discussion above, in which I drew out the need to nourish oneself and which explored ways of nurturing the non-conscious in order to feed creative activity, that the forms of professional development which support creativity are likely to be broad.

On one level, there is no reason to suppose that forms of professional development activity (or CPD: continuing professional development) appropriate to fostering creativity should be any different to other forms of CPD. Thus, methods are likely to include:

- action-research;
- self-directed study;
- using distance-learning materials;
- receiving on-the-job coaching, mentoring or tutoring;
- school-based and off-site courses of various lengths;
- job-shadowing and rotation;
- membership of a working party or task group;
- teacher placement;
- personal reflection;
- experiential 'assignments';
- collaborative learning.

(Craft, 1996a: 7)

On another level, however, it seems to me likely that CPD designed to foster creativity will have three major differences.

First, it is likely to involve some form of interaction with feedback, enabling the teacher to get into relationship with others, to give and receive feedback and to explore dynamics of fostering or blocking the creativity of others.

Second, it is likely to involve a range of opportunities for accessing the non-conscious both for the teacher and for learners in their care (some teachers may find meditation forms an important part of their CPD, for example).

And, third, since my thesis is that the teacher needs to feel nourished in order to stimulate the creativity of learners, it needs to be chosen and opted into by the individual. Clearly, each individual will be attracted to a unique profile of forms of CPD. No one particular profile is 'the correct way', just as there is no one 'correct way' to teach; personal style and professional artistry are influential and necessary elements in the mix, affecting the shape of the outcome.

So, what should professional development for fostering creativity focus upon in terms of content?

The nature of creativity

Clearly, some exploration of the nature of creativity must form part of professional development for creativity. As indicated in Chapter 1, the National Committee on Creative and Cultural Education (1999: 29) describes creativity as 'imaginative activity fashioned so as to yield an outcome that is of value as well as original'. Thus, an exploration of what is meant by imaginative activity, value and originality is essential. I have suggested some interpretations of each in Chapter 1. And, as discussed in both Chapters 1 and 2, in my own formulation of creativity I set these notions of value and originality in the context of possibility thinking, and within a framework of people, processes and domains.

Management and creativity

CPD for fostering creativity also needs to address classroom and group management and other classroom strategies. Enabling individuals to exercise possibility thinking can at times seem in tension with managing a large (or even a small) group of learners. For there will inevitably be limits to the extent to which it is possible to encourage the freedom and autonomy in thinking and expression for the individual in the context of a classroom. Finding the delicate balance between fostering the creativity of each individual such that others are not 'squashed' is a matter of professional judgement. This is, of course, a tension which has puzzled political scientists for centuries.

I want to suggest that encouraging all individuals in the classroom to be 'in relationship' with others may be important in enabling all and crushing none. This notion was introduced in Chapter 7.

Relationships in schools

Being in relationship with others in the school community may involve children and adults recognising and acknowledging one another's experiences, ideas and perspectives. It means involving all children and all categories of staff. Being in relationship in the context of creativity involves, it seems to me, a spectrum of possibilities.

At one end, creativity may in some instances be the product of being in relationship with others (in this sense an idea or an outcome may be co-created). Co-creation does not necessarily mean collaboration, however, although it may at times involve working together. Thus somewhere further along the spectrum of being in relationship, co-creation may involve minimal input from others, for the knowledge that others may potentially relate to the idea or outcome may be sufficient stimulus to enable an individual to create. At the other end of the spectrum, an individually produced creative outcome may involve the stimulus to relate to others, or to find out how the idea or outcome 'lands'.

It is not a simple 'map'; different circumstances make varying demands; and individuals have preferred styles of working as Belbin (1981) and others have documented. Indeed, Gardner's (1993b) work on creativity suggests that highly creative individuals often need to be 'on the edge' of a group, a field or an activity, and that collaborating closely with others crushes their creative capacity. Perhaps what is important here is that individuals need different mixes of circumstances, across time and context as well as task.

Adult staff may offer one another feedback on their practice, by observing as 'critical friends'; what in some professions, for example social work, is called 'supervision'. Just as adults in the school's community can be critical friends to one another in offering feedback on ways of developing their practice, so children may too.

Framing and reframing practice

All of the elements of professional development discussed so far form a part of the discourse of both framing and reframing practice in order to foster creativity. Included, therefore, in the focus of CPD needs to be the notion of describing and analysing practice, in order to develop practices which foster creativity in children.

Barriers to professional development for creativity

All change and development throws up resistance as well as excitement and enthusiasm; resistance can be one form of barrier to professional development. So, what is behind it?

The complexity of the role of the teacher and breadth of the job are two commonly cited reasons for resistance. Others include the general overload of the job, change fatigue and cynicism stemming from perceptions of and experience of external judgement/inducements such as Ofsted inspection and TTA criteria. If creativity is perceived, erroneously, as a new curriculum subject rather than an aspect of all subjects which enables mastery, then curriculum overload is another reason cited for not wanting to develop with this in mind. Schools are, also, conservative places, as Hargreaves has argued (1994). Some teachers feel, with some reason, that schools are not places where creativity can be encouraged. The work of Holt (1991) documents some of the reasons for this (the need to manage being dominant, often over inspiration; the shift of perspective from the individual to the collective in the mind of the teaching caucus; the emphasis on teaching rather than on learning). Perhaps many teachers feel, too, that since their own individuality and creativity is suppressed in some ways within a school setting, it is difficult for them to feel wholehearted in their attempts to foster these in others.

There are no easy answers to such barriers, although schools trying to foster creativity will struggle to do so in a coherent way unless all staff 'sign up' to the principle of doing so. The story of Jamie's patchwork of experiences as he learned with a diverse set of teachers and expectations in his inner London primary school will be a familiar one to many teachers:

Jamie did not go to nursery school but was at home until he started primary school when he was 4. He is now 11, and in Year 6; this is his last year before going to secondary school.

When he began school in the Reception class, Jamie spent the mornings learning through projects and the afternoons choosing. Sometimes they did PE, or science, or RE, or number work and that was usually outside the project. The teacher used to show the children how to do each task and then they would try it for themselves. She gave shiny gold stars to children who did their morning work really well. She liked it when the children lined up in twos neatly and when they sat up straight on the mat.

In Year 1, Jamie found that he was learning mathematics, science, technology and English in the mornings. His teacher gave his group (green) special work to do in each subject, and when they had finished they could choose from the puzzles and table top games which she had laid out on their table, until playtime or lunch time. In the afternoons he learned history and geography and singing (there was a piano in the room which his teacher knew how to play). He had a special book for each subject and he sat with the green table for nearly everything. When he had finished in the afternoons, he could choose between playing with puzzles, construction material, or in the sand or water or shop, painting, modelling or reading. His teacher liked it when they got the answers right in maths and got lots of ticks.

In Year 2, Jamie was learning through projects again except for maths, which was done on sheets of paper which the children then had to put in the teacher's tray for marking (though often he never saw his sheets of paper again). This time he sat at different tables at different times (he couldn't work out which group he would be in and when). So, in some ways this was a confusing year. On the other hand, this teacher was very keen to hear whatever the children wanted to say. She was always asking them to give her a different idea or a new answer, which she might not be expecting. From that point of view it was an exciting year.

In Year 3, Jamie learned through one project each half term and kept all his work for the project in his tray. At the end of the project his teacher made him choose work to put in his own special project book. He had a red book with squares in it for mathematics and sometimes the teacher gave the children problem solving investigations to have a go at in maths too. He really liked the technology parts of the projects with that teacher. The teacher had a computer in the classroom all the time and taught the children how to use the e-mail system. He organised pen pals with a class of children in America and Jamie really enjoyed writing to his, once a fortnight. That teacher was really keen on cricket and football and was really good at teaching those, but Jamie had the feeling that his teacher didn't really like some of the sitting down work quite so much. One of the really good things about that year was they were allowed to get up and move about the room and make quite a lot of noise, unlike in the next year.

In Year 4, the teacher did lots of work on the board and had different corners of the room for technology, English, maths, etc. Jamie had different books for each subject and also a draft book which he had to write a lot of his work in first. He was not allowed to get up from his table without permission and the class worked in silence. But their teacher had a great sense of humour and encouraged the children to have private jokes with her. She was strict, but she seemed to understand what made each person tick. Jamie enjoyed that year although he didn't like not being allowed to get up and move about. It was a good year for thinking.

In Year 5 there were lots of projects, a history one, a geography one and a technology one. His teacher wrote on the board what to do each morning for each group and Jamie never ran out of things to do. They could choose the order in which they were done. Everyone was expected to complete their work within a specified time and then there would be extension activities. Jamie thought that was quite good, as he felt trusted to work at his own pace, but he also felt encouraged to go fast and both of those were a good thing, he thought. The work he was given was always just right and he was able to carry on thinking from the year before, as this teacher was quite keen on getting to know everyone really well, too.

Now he is in Year 6, Jamie has a book for each subject and his teacher tells him exactly what to write in each one. This teacher is definitely not interested in what the children have to say. There are right answers for almost everything and the teacher knows what they are. He says the children are big now and ready to go to secondary school where they will have to be sensible and quiet. All of this is quite frustrating as Jamie had got used to having his own ideas and telling them to other people, as well as hearing ideas from other children in his class. But this teacher is good at football and all of the children have learned very quickly how to sit in complete silence for most of each lesson. Jamie has a special sign language which he uses to signal his friend who sits on the other side of the room (their tables are organised in a horse-shoe shape with the teacher at the front).

(Based on a real primary school in Islington, North London and a real child, whose name has been altered for this case study)

In the recent past, commentators and researchers have noted that primary teachers have seen themselves as relatively autonomous and having little influence over the school as a whole and its policies; as Campbell put it, 'teachers first and members of a school second' (Campbell, 1985: 20). This may be less true now than it has been in the past, in that the National Curriculum and arrangements for assessment have forced teachers to work together more coherently within the school. However, I have included the case study since it demonstrates that even post-National Curriculum, working cohesively does not just 'happen' because teachers are working in the same school. Indeed, Nias (1989) and Pollard (1985) have documented, through their ethnographic explorations of the dominant cultures in primary staffrooms, that proximity may simply result in sweeping differences in opinion and practice 'under the carpet' and finding common areas about which to agree. Although children are resilient to discontinuities and indeed there are some positives in having a variation in expectations throughout a school, I would argue creativity is a special case. Like a volcano once it has erupted, the 'lid' cannot easily be put back on – and indeed why should it be?

There are particular challenges, too, in considering appropriate ways of involving non-teaching staff in supporting children's 'possibility thinking'. Consider how teaching assistants, lunch time supervisors, kitchen staff, office staff, the school keeper and cleaning staff could be involved in fostering the possibility thinking of all pupils in the school. Being open to possibility does not necessarily mean failing to manage a classroom, having a fluid and uncontrolled curriculum, taking forever over a small task or running away with a 'distraction' brought in by a child for the rest of the day. Perhaps the most significant aspect of possibility thinking is starting from the foundation of expecting children to diverge, to do it differently or to be original – rather than to converge or to conform. It should be immediately obvious that some roles in the school community may involve more tasks relating to encouraging conformity than others do. To what extent is conformity necessary for the good of all? In which contexts is it more necessary, and in which less? Discovering the appropriate balance between management and creativity, as indicated earlier, but with *all* staff, is a challenge facing all schools or other learning institutions.

There are, occasionally, barriers to creativity which come from the children themselves; if learners are exhausted or hungry, or simply preoccupied. Like anything else in teaching and learning, asking children to be creative needs to be carefully timed and well supported. Aside from ensuring that children's basic needs for food and rest are being met, partnership with the home is another significant element of fostering creativity, since a teacher who fosters chidren's creativity may be asking for more divergence than some families may be used to. Thus, sharing the notion of possibility thinking and its purposes as well as its challenges with carers and parents is important – and this is another perspective on CPD for fostering creativity.

Professionally developing the system

Perhaps the largest barriers to fostering creativity in schools are to do with the nature of the current educating system itself. In Chapter 10, I explore some systems issues in educating for creativity, which needs re-visioning by those who know most about it, who live, breathe and work in it.

Summing up

In this chapter, I have explored practical aspects of reframing practice in order to give greater priority to fostering creativity. I have focused on the professional development issues in particular.

Drawing on the research project introduced in Chapter 7, I looked at aspects of nurturing one's own self-esteem as a teacher, looking at risk-taking, the need for openness and receptivity and practical strategies for drawing the non-conscious into the conscious, suggesting that nurturing oneself in this way is a little like building a compost heap, or 'mulching'.

I went on to consider forms and foci for professional development, suggesting that the role of the non-conscious, meeting individuals' needs and also interactivity are likely to influence the choice of CPD method. I looked at the nature of creativity, management and creativity, relationships and the notion of reframing as important topics for CPD.

Finally I explored some possible barriers to CPD for creativity, arguing that despite inevitable resistance it is important for teachers and schools to work together in finding ways of fostering it, since creativity is a life skill which children are going to need more and more of in the twenty-first century.

In the next chapter, I go on to look at system wide issues in fostering creativity and ask what kind of learning systems are appropriate for the young people of the twenty-first century.

Acknowledgements

I would like to thank all of the educators with whom I have worked in south-east England, and whose practice has informed this chapter. Also Tom Lyons, my co-researcher on the London project, Christine Kimberley and Jana Dugal, formerly of the Institute for Creativity. Thanks also to Clare Hurley, my lifelong friend, co-student and colleague, whose perspective on children and creativity in classrooms and homes has been illuminating.

Part IV
Vision

10 Re-visioning education for the twenty-first century

This chapter forms an exploration of 're-engineering' or 'doing it differently' at the level of the education systems in place for educating. Included is some discussion of blocks to creativity.

Taking stock

At the end of the twentieth century, it is timely to ask what sorts of systems might be appropriate for educating children in the future. The coming of the year 2000 provides a psychological 'new leaf' – an opportunity, albeit an artificial one, to ask whether a 'sweep out' of the old needs to happen, and if so, how. Educational researchers and commentators are already starting to ask such questions and to pose possible scenarios in answer (Bentley, 1998). Before looking at some of the 'answers' offered, however, I want to look first at the context for change and then at some of the barriers to it.

Changes in technology, particularly information and communication technologies, mean a transformation in ways in which children can learn, and a multiplication of settings in which learning can be facilitated, too. Learners – adults and children alike – can access a vast and growing database of information on self-chosen topics, within moments and in a learner-directed way, via the information superhighway. Although there are currently in England inequalities in access to such information, in terms of both wealth and gender, these are rapidly altering as the scope of the technology develops and values in society alter in relation to what it can offer. Government initiatives such as the National Grid for Learning (1998) support such changes in learning patterns by linking public libraries to the Internet and setting up learning 'clubs' such as GridClub, through which children as young as 7 can play a variety of games involving general knowledge. As the information explosion continues, knowledge (distinct from information in that it is refined, considered, interpreted) is restructured. Learning communities form and re-form in the electronic medium and pure information is transformed into new forms of shared, public knowledge.

The changes in information and communication technology also bring enormous possibilities to schools as institutions, and open many doors to how children may be supported in learning in the future, as I began to explore in Chapter 6. Initiatives such as the Open University's Learning Schools Programme are exploring the possibilities of technology for teaching and learning, at the level of preparing teachers of both primary- and secondary-aged children, and also librarians, to implement it. This particular school-focused initiative, in partnership with Research Machines and funded by the government over several years as part of its commitment to the National Grid for Learning, focuses on the individual teachers, their ICT needs and practice in the context of their particular schools. A school-based supported open learning programme, it aims to:

- Provide the capability for teachers to decide when to use appropriate ICT activities in their teaching to enhance the learning of their students and develop the curriculum;
- Enable teachers to plan lessons using ICT, and to be able to reflect on the implementation of these plans;
- Enable teachers to draw up an action plan that will specify further training needed, actions to be taken in the curriculum and any implications for the school (e.g. purchase of software), all of which will be included in School Development Plans.

(McCormick, 1998: 1)

Thus in its training format (independent and interactive, multi-media open learning), the project models some of the skills it will develop in teachers' ICT capability. It could be argued that as well as bringing with it the technology for independent learning, the end of the twentieth century also brings with it an increased need for this.

Individual and corporate creativity/imagination have now become a topic of study by cognitive psychologists, philosophers, educationalists and management experts alike (Stern, 1992). As argued in this book, the end of the twentieth century is witnessing a massive shift in attitude to and importance of creativity and imagination in everyday lives and domains of knowledge. We need transformation, at both personal and system level.

Challenges – inner and outer

It could be argued that one of the biggest challenges to fostering creativity at either the personal or the system level is the attitude which begins with 'yes, but'. In Chapter 9, I considered some of the blocks which may arise toward professional development focused on supporting creativity. In this chapter I shall explore first some possible internal inhibitors to creativity and then some possible wider social ones, in order to go on to look at systems-level strategies for change.

Challenges to creativity from within oneself

Learned habits may, at times, inhibit us. And at times, what we value may be precisely what we do not need. Shallcross (1981: 65–6) suggests the following internal inhibitors:

- assumed expectations of other people;
- failure to be aware of all available information;
- lack of effort or laziness;
- assumed or self-imposed boundaries or limitations;
- mind sets;
- rigidity or inflexibility . . . ;
- fear of failure or of taking risks;
- conformity or fear of appearing to be different;
- fear of ridicule;
- reliance on authority or following patterns of behaviour set by others;
- routine;
- comfort;
- familiarity;
- a need for things to be orderly all the time;
- superstition and acceptance of fate, heredity or one's station in life.

(Shallcross, 1981: 65–66)

This list includes overlapping and repeating items, and is not, of course, exhaustive. To it might be added other possibilities:

- a belief that life cannot be different;
- inexperience in acknowledging existing achievements;
- cynicism, or practised refusal/inflexibility;
- fear of not being good enough;
- lack of practice in making choices;
- fear of change;
- a wish to control;
- addictions including workaholism;
- discomfort with the consequences of change;
- lack of awareness of how others perceive one's actions.

Internal inhibitors are not the only ones we face, particularly when contemplating the possible system-level change, introduced earlier in the chapter. The global, transnational and national society context for our creative impulses toward systemic transformation is a complex and contradictory one.

Challenges to creativity from society: contradictions

We might expect creativity to be consciously suppressed in certain contexts in that it involves asking questions. Egan (1992) has charted ways in which, historically, creativity has indeed been suppressed at the level of society. His analysis of the marginalisation of imagination and creativity demonstrates ways in which imagination and creativity have, since the time of the ancient Greeks, represented a 'rebellion against divine order' (1992: 13). Thus, he argues, the notion 'in the imagination' has attracted disapproval and has been considered to be a mimicking of divine capability. The Romantic imagination reversed some of the negativity associated with imagination and creativity through the development of the Romantic Arts. Nevertheless, the centrality of imagination and creativity in all domains of knowledge and for all people, rather than solely the arts, has only toward the end of the twentieth century become critical to everyday lives.

We live in a society of contradictions: on the one hand, choice, possibility, change and growth are seen as necessary and overtly encouraged. Our existence revolves around what Smart (1993) has called 'relational values' rather than absolute ones, partly because of the continual state of flux in which society exists.

On the other hand, there is an increase in uniformity at the level of the market, as Ritzer (1993) has identified, in what he has called 'McDonaldization', in other words, the domination of homogeneous products, work routines and technologies such as one finds in the McDonald's hamburger chain. With this increase in uniformity comes a set of rigidly adhered to organisational values and rules – indeed there is even a McDonald's University, which teaches employees the values and beliefs of the chain.

It has been argued (Craft, 1995) that there is some parallel between the values-uniformity implied within the McDonald's set up and chains like it, and the discernible political attempt to control and hold still within education. The modes of doing so include the centralised school curriculum and arrangements for assessing learning of it, and an increased emphasis on managerialism, which is well documented (Avis *et al.*, 1996).

If we look at creativity in education, then, we see a need, on the one hand, for teachers to become increasingly experts in fostering creativity and, on the other, an attempt to crush all artistry from the profession and to reduce teaching to a technicist activity.

The fragmentary nature of our post-modern existence means that in many ways the mores and shared traditions are mixed and confused. Multiple possibilities exist for us in adopting, for example, spiritual, social, economic and technological identities and actions. In many arenas we have no models to follow and are having to work out what the possibilities are as we go along. The family is an example. Around 40 per cent of children now live in families where one parent has found a new partnership. That is nearly half of all children, who now belong to, or have experience of, more than one family.

Other society level challenges to creativity and vision include the role and mode of communications – the mass media. Gammage (1996) has spoken of the tendency of the mass media to 'gobbetize' information – it could also be argued that the media is capable of misinformation, purely by dint of what is left out, and the simplistic ways in which complex issues are presented.

For example, during a trip to New York just before Christmas in the mid-1990s, I was struck at the inclusion on television news of an item concerning the shortage of 'Tickle me Elmo' cuddly toys in stores across the USA. This was lead story on several news bulletins, alongside the hostages being held at that time in the Japanese embassy in Peru. The question raised for me was why this sales story was considered to be news at all. Personal perspectives on any current affairs story such as this news item represent a variety of different and contradictory positions, reflecting a range of values, including cynical, 'naive', descriptive, positive, appreciative, etc. So, when I shared my interpretation with a group of educators, we identified a range of responses to it, including the following:

- news items like that are specially designed to draw in child viewers – it is a commercial gimmick;
- news has to support sales in the United States, unlike here;
- maybe there was no other big news story that day;
- it's good entertainment;
- sales in America means success;
- all children have the right to have stories which affect them represented in adult news programmes;
- Christmas is about sales;
- TV must tell domestic news stories.

The 'Tickle Me Elmo' story also highlights another contradiction. Television is an immensely creative form of mass media, in both its presentation and the effect which it has on viewers. However, it has the potential to simplify and misrepresent. Although it is a medium capable of stimulating creative, thoughtful responses, it has the potential to close down debate entirely. The same phenomenon can be observed in the film industry, in glossy magazines, in tabloid (and to a lesser extent, broadsheet) newspapers, and in the booming CD-ROM marketplace.

The deification of the market is another of the contradictions which we live with. Innovation is critical to increased competitiveness in business. The challenge is to invent, re-package or re-conceptualise ideas and products just as the previous one peaks, with the result that we are sucked into a continuous cycle of invention and sale. Thus living in a market economy where goods are bought and sold on the basis of want rather than need, with market values determined by factors such as scarcity and abundance, drives us to a need for creative activity. Skinner (1996) has called the constant need for innovation in the workplace 'mentafacture' – production by brain – and 'stylofacture' – the production of lifestyle possibilities. Innovation in this context can be seen as the successful exploitation of new ideas.

And yet, as the marketplace drives this creative activity it can also dull our capability to see beyond the framework of values in which we are innovating. It makes it more difficult for us to see the impact of our innovations on the globe, its peoples, creatures, seascapes, landscapes and vegetation. So, the values of our society can be seen as providing both inducements and barriers to creating and, more importantly, to the ways in which we perceive our creations.

Summing up so far

I have suggested that our underpinning beliefs about our personal lives and the society which surrounds us may foster or block our own creativity.

I have discussed some possible personal and societal sources of learned habits which suppress creativity, including some of the contradictions of post-modern living.

As part of this discussion I have examined the fragmentation and multiple possibilities in our lives, played out in many arenas. This co-exists with the contrasting consolidation of fundamentalism and uniformity in each of these arenas.

In the next part of the chapter I look at some of the practical challenges involved in transforming education through vision, ultimately at the level of the systems we have in place for educating.

Vision and transformation at the system level

Education greatly needs vision. As Michael Barber (1996) eloquently puts it, we are faced with global challenge, as well as moral collapse and confusion. In addition, we are faced with anxieties about how well educated our young people are (outside the top 20 per cent of young people, that is) when they leave school, and the level of basic literacy of adults.

Such problems form part of yet another set of contradictions; they lie alongside 'successes', which include much higher achievement in GCSEs, A levels and GNVQs, the increasing trend of girls out-performing boys at all levels, as well as higher staying-on rates (though these are balanced against changes in the economy which mean jobs are scarce and incentives to leave full-time education are therefore fewer than they were).

A further contradiction is that alongside the increased staying-on rates, more and more children, particularly boys in their early teens onward, are truanting from school, or being excluded. Indeed as Tim Brighouse, Chief Education Officer of Birmingham, pointed out, as long ago as the 1994 Council of Local Authorities Conference,

> the pattern of exclusion, having been almost exclusively confined to Year 11 (age sixteen) youngsters ten years ago, has shifted first to Year 11 and Year 10, then to Year 11, Year 10 and Year 9, and finally until now there is a strong representation of years 11, 10, 9 and 8 among those permanently excluded from the school in which they were originally enrolled in Year 7. Moreover, the overall numbers have escalated through that 10-year period.

As Barber (1996) has noted, alongside the truanting, or the 'disappeared' are the disaffected. Quoting from the Keele University surveys of 30,000 children in secondary schools, he claims that pupil disruption, bullying and noise affect a third of respondents. He suggests

> it is necessary to reach the depressing conclusion that a minority, perhaps 10–15 per cent nationally, but much more numerous in some particular schools, are disrupting education for the majority of pupils and impairing the quality of teacher–pupil relationships throughout many schools.
>
> (Barber, 1996: 78–79)

He also points out that boredom and lack of motivation affect huge numbers of children.

Although the Keele data is from secondary education, I use it here to emphasise that we need a form of educating which enables all children to exercise imagination and creativity through engaged learning throughout their schooling and in a way which has relevance to their lives, now and in the future. Can you with all certainty say that all of the children with whom you have contact feel motivated and that school is relevant for them? We have a need to jump beyond the cultural revolution which was imposed on schools in the late 1980s, and beyond the institutional constraints formed by the type of mass-schooling system which we operate as part of now, to something which is more likely to equip learners for the uncertainties and skill demands in life.

Developing and designing systems

Social systems design is a new focus in world-wide thinking about how to develop systems. Initiated by Banathy (1991), Senior Research Director in educational research and development and also Emeritus Professor of Systems Science in California, it has much to offer to the development of education systems in England.

Over the last fifty years or so, systems thinking and practice has been used to lead the analysis and solution of complex management and organisational problems. The new approach, named by its proponents 'systems design', involves the development, initially within small communities (such as the family, school, local community) and ultimately within larger ones (the locality, the country, the global community), of a vision of what the collective grouping desire; what Ackoff (1981) calls an Ideal vision. The idea is that the Ideal is 'co-designed' or 'co-created'. One of the core principles of systems design is that it facilitates all individuals in being active participants in the design of their own lives.

As argued elsewhere (Dyer and Craft, 1997), social systems design seems to offer a powerful tool for education. Social systems design offers the opportunity to 're-vision' what education is for, in contrast to revising or reforming it. The principles of systems design offer a way of developing a learning and human development system which is based on a contrasting set of assumptions from the ones currently in use.

Systems thinking is an organic model for envisioning the future. It involves:

- the development of a new vision by collective action by communities (such as social units, clubs, schools, associations, etc.);
- each individual member co-designing, or co-creating, with others – in this way participating actively in their own life-design;
- harnessing everyone's creative ability and not just that of the elite; and
- building relationships between people and their world.

(Dyer and Craft, 1997: 91)

. . . and it involves a culture change in fostering vision in education.

Asking different questions

We are continually changing and reforming education. As argued elsewhere (Dyer and Craft, 1997), we tend to use 'old' questions, such as the following ones, to fix what we currently have:

- what is wrong with the system?
- how can we improve it?, restructure it?
- how can we provide more teaching time?
- how can we decrease class size so pupils get more teacher attention?
- how can we improve behaviour?
- how can we improve pupil, teacher and school performance?
- how can we get more support from our school governors?
- how can we increase achievement in mathematics so that pupils' achievements compare favourably with those of children in Pacific Rim countries?
- how can we increase achievement in reading?
- how can we increase achievement in the sciences and technology so we as a nation can compete better in the economic arena?

(Dyer and Craft, 1997: 92)

These are, of course, important questions. However, they involve two weaknesses. First, they assume a simple relationship of cause and effect between education and society at large and, second, they leave no scope for questioning the forms of education provision. Up until now, such questions have driven reform, which has accepted current forms of education provision for young children, i.e. play groups, pre-schools and schools. Yet, these may not be the most appropriate forms for the political, social, economic and spiritual transience which characterises the end of the twentieth century. The growing numbers of parents choosing to educate at home, some of whom were represented at a recent Open University conference on home education,[1] may be an indication of the challenge facing society.

Questions for an information age

The move to a post-industrial 'information age' has created enormous transformations and discontinuities in all aspects of our lives; requiring change in the way we think about learning and the ways we perceive the social function of education. As indicated in the introduction to this chapter, ultimately the shift requires us to think differently about provision of learning arrangements.

As proposed elsewhere (Dyer and Craft, 1997), appropriate questions could include:

–   What is the nature and what are the characteristics of the emerging post-industrial information/knowledge age?
–   What are the educational implications of those characteristics?
–   What framework can we use to re-think education and what vision, core ideas and core values might inspire our thinking?

(Dyer and Craft, 1997: 93)

Characteristics of organisations in the future, which would include those concerned with education, may be influenced by the changing paradigm for organisational characteristics. The emerging paradigm values the following principles in organisations: fluidity, flexibility, dynamism, evolutionary development, and enabling processes for both individuals and the collective.

Practical steps toward the development of the Ideal vision have been developed by Dyer (Dyer, 1995; Dyer and Craft, 1997). Based on the three steps of 'transcendence, re-visioning and transformation', this approach draws in all of those involved in an organisation and is suitable for institutions such as schools. Vision and co-creation are needed at a much more systemic level. But facilitating these in ways which enable individuals to have their own voices heard, and which allow the representation of different sets of interests, and thus in ways which can truly be called 'co-creative' is a significant social challenge. The attitude and skill involved in co-creation has been named the fifth 'literacy' (Banathy, 1992 and 1996) to add alongside the original 3 R's, and computer literacy.

Another characteristic of thinking creatively about any topic, including education, is that it involves not doing it more, but doing it differently. It seems to me that we need to go beyond 'improvement' or 'effectiveness'. In terms of creativity, we need to look beyond fostering creative approaches for the same ends, to how we could do it differently, at whatever level we are working.

There are plenty of suggestions already around. For example, proposals from Barber and Brighouse for long-term associateships from the local community, in order to help keep teachers up to date with change in knowledge and its application, and the need to provide more teaching assistants at the level of 'para-professionals', the possibility of learning accounts for teachers and much more flexible times and places of work for teachers and pupils (Barber and Brighouse, 1992).

Barber (1996) has proposed the 'Individual Learning Promise' which should be a commitment to learning agreed through a partnership of the pupil, the school and the pupil's parents, where the individual's progress is planned, implemented and reviewed. Small independent centres such as the New Learning Centre in North London are already working on these lines, alongside schools.

A more radical scenario is proposed by Bentley (1998), who calls for neighbourhood lifelong learning centres, intimately related to the local businesses and communities, in which individuals could pursue learning in an experiential way, using a variety of resources, in a self-directed fashion. He emphasises the potential of such learning centres to foster 'agency' and the taking of personal responsibility in individual children, which means the education professionals giving up some control over where, when and how each learner learns.

Adcock (1994), too, has suggested a model of teaching and learning based on the personal tutor supported by media resource centres, and personal choice on the part of children. Meighan (1997) has suggested home learning is a powerful precursor to the next learning system. Thousands of parents are now educating their children at home, supported in the UK by organisations such as Education Otherwise. Education at home is increasingly common in Europe, North America and also in Australasia, and this is well documented (Thomas, 1994b, 1998; Meighan, 1995). There is increasing evidence that early intellectual development happens through everyday conversations (Tizard and Hughes, 1984; Rogoff, 1990). According to research undertaken by Thomas (1992, 1994a), formalised teaching sessions for children educated in the home seem to have little difference in effectiveness from the 'natural apprenticeship' model which tends to be used in infancy. The suggestion from Thomas's work is that to be effective, learning may not need to take place in the 'classroom'. And as Meighan (1995) documents, the intellectual achievement and social skills of home-educated children are repeatedly demonstrated to be excellent.

Elsewhere, I have proposed, with Dugal (Craft and Dugal, 1997), a vision of a system of education which has something in common with Bentley's, introduced above. In my vision, education would co-exist with free day care from 8 a.m. until 7 p.m., in which children would have an entitlement to learn (and the resource to support it; a notion also proposed by the National Commission on Education, 1995), and also far more choice about what, how and when they undertook it, and thus they would enter into learning contracts of finite length. Consequently the job of being a teacher would involve much greater flexibility, and probably smaller numbers of pupils.

A similar model is proposed by Barber (1996) who suggests

> Policy makers will need to begin to think of education as having three strands:
> - learning at school;
> - learning in organised out-of-school locations; and
> - learning at home.
>
> (Barber, 1996: 259)

The point is, we need to do it differently.

At the heart of the need to do it differently rather than doing it more, is the idea summed up in this old Hebrew proverb:

> Do not confine your children to your own learning for they were born in another time.

> (Meighan, 1994)

We need a new paradigm for creating vision in education, which allows us to step outside of the contradictions to a space which enables us to create with vision, from compassion. It means applying our creativity to create new frameworks. It could mean co-creating, as suggested in this chapter. It could also involve drawing on our creative impulses from a different level. In the next chapter, I explore the notion of trusting what is 'implicate', a term coined by scientists Bohm and Peat (1989).

Summing up: developing vision in education

I have introduced a social systems design approach to fostering change at the macro level, along with some of the values implicit within it. These include co-creation.

I have suggested that what we need in education is to 'do it differently' rather than 'doing it more'. We need to foster a new vision, to go beyond 'improvement' to looking at how we might educate in a different way or ways. I mentioned some which have already been proposed.

I suggested that social systems design offers a possible process by which such re-engineering in education might take place in a way which is co-creative.

The notion of 're-engineering' (Hammer and Champy, 1993) rather than 'reform' is one which I explore further as part of Chapter 11.

Acknowledgements

This chapter is a development of two, originally written with Jana Dugal and Gordon Dyer respectively, for one of my previous books, *Can You Teach Creativity?*, published in 1997 by Education Now. My thanks to these two individuals for their co-creativity, vision and inspiration.

Notes

1   An activity of the Open University Creativity in Education Community which is facilitated by Anna Craft and Bob Jeffrey at The Open University School of Education. For information, write to either of the above at The Open University School of Education, Walton Hall, Milton Keynes, MK7 6AA.

11 Creativity, virtue and humanity

In this chapter, I propose creativity as a post-modern virtue. I relate the roles of education in the twenty-first century, to the fostering of creative decision making and the need for personal autonomy in learners, emphasising the need for education to foster compassion and humanity. I go on to consider aspects of 'vision', exploring briefly the notion of re-engineering education, again setting the creative action of the individual in the context of the whole.

Time is short and the task is urgent. Auschwitz is the prime example of what happens when technology is harnessed to evil. Evil is real. So is good. There is a choice and we are not so much chosen as choosers. Life is holy. All life, mine and yours and that of those who came before us and the life of those after us.

(Hugo Gryn, 1930–1996)

These words, spoken by Rabbi Hugo Gryn in the context of his inclusive approach to inter-faith tolerance, have direct relevance to creativity. For creating does not take place in a vacuum free of values. Invention is not, *of itself*, good. As human beings we are also capable of creating ideas and technologies which destroy others and our wider environment. Our classrooms and learning spaces need to foster learners' abilities to understand and evaluate the values which underpin their own creativity and that of others. And we need to enable children to reflect critically upon these. As Hugo Gryn's words imply, this means acknowledging the wider environment, and all it contains.

Creativity as a post-modern virtue

Discussions in philosophy of education of 'the virtues', stem from Aristotle's work. Aristotle regarded human life as being about the pursuit of ends (Ross, Ackrill and Urmson, 1980). He spent his energies in discovering the nature of the end or ends at which people ought to aim. The end of human life must be chosen for its own sake and something that is itself satisfying. Human 'good' for Aristotle was about 'good moral activity' or 'good intellectual activity'.

He distinguished between intellectual and moral virtue. Intellectual virtue comes about through teaching, whereas moral virtue comes about through habit. The notion of a virtue indicates a disposition of character, state of character, not a 'passion' (appetite, fear, confidence, envy, joy, friendly feeling, hatred, longing, emulation, pity, pleasure/pain) or a 'faculty' (ways in which we are capable of feeling the passions).

Aristotle suggested a number of virtues which were necessary to live the good life. These were:

- courage;
- temperance;
- 'pride';
- justice (universal, particular, i.e. distribution of honour or profit, rectificatory justice and reciprocal justice);
- excellences of the intellect (five states through which we reach truth: science, art, practical wisdom, intuitive wisdom and theoretical wisdom);
- goodness (heroic and divine, continence and virtue; continence is about rationality, temperance and self-control, whereas incontinence is associated with various pleasures and pains, including those not controllable by rationality);
- friendship.

According to Aristotle, pleasure in doing 'virtuous acts' indicates that 'the virtuous disposition has been acquired'. The ideal to aim for is 'the mean disposition', which involves neither excess nor deficiency.

Underpinning all of the virtues which Aristotle named was the notion of 'moral virtue'. The implication of 'moral virtue' is that action is done by choice, arrived at through intentional deliberation. For Aristotle, the well-being of humankind was an activity rather than a state. It was desirable for its own sake. For him, well-being was about living the contemplative life. In different books this seems to mean different things, including metaphysics, mathematics, and the study of nature (in the *Metaphysics*); also contemplation of beauty and religious contemplation – and the study and serving of God (the *Eumadian Ethics*).

The idea of the virtue as an essential activity in enabling the living of life in a particular era has been taken up by philosophers through the ages. For example, as Carr (1991) has described, Rousseau examined the notion of virtue as self-determination. Indeed in his *Emile*, he is concerned as Carr puts it, 'to trace the development of the totally unprejudiced, reasonable and free agent' (p. 71).

The pivotal notion that individuals are capable of *choice* after some deliberation over what actions they in fact take, which Aristotle's writings encompassed, is present in Rousseau's writing, as well as within the ideas of much more recent philosophers attempting to translate Aristotelian ideas into post-modern life (Hardie, 1980; Tobin, 1989).

One significant aspect of very recent discussions of the Aristotelian notion of 'virtue' is the recognition of the role of the intuitive in Aristotle's own writing

(Hardie, 1980) and also of the affective in moral decision making, again implicit in Aristotle's writing (Tobin, 1989). These are elements which I accord a role in 'little c' creativity, as indicated in Chapters 1 and 2.

More importantly, however, I want to suggest 'little c' creativity as a possible 'virtue' for a post-modern age – in other words, as a contributor to well-being, when framed in ethical context. For, as indicated by the quotation from Rabbi Hugo Gryn at the start of this chapter, creativity may be used for both constructive and destructive ends.

A romantic ideal

Perhaps inevitably, any discussion of 'virtue' provides a reflection of and commentary on what is deemed necessary for life in any particular political context. In my discussion of creativity I am, similarly, attempting to articulate a particular social 'Ideal', which enables people to both survive in and make sense of the chaos of choice and identity which characterises life in the post-modern world, which others have written about elsewhere (Edwards, 1995; Kellner, 1992; Ritzer, 1993; Smart, 1993).

In relating this Ideal for social life to existing political theory, there may be connections with the Romantic, anti-Enlightenment theories of political and artistic life, and also to liberal notions such as those proposed by Berlin during the twentieth century (Gray, 1995).

First, the Romantic movement. The commitment of the Romantic, counter-Enlightenment thinkers to originality is also core to my conception of creativity as discussed in Chapter 1 – although originality in 'little c' creativity is unlikely to involve reference to a broad field of activity in the same way as originality in a Romantic painter's work such as, for example, Turner.

Taking action is a key part of 'little c' creativity. It is a similar notion to the 'expressivist' one expressed by Taylor (1989) in his discussion of the Romantic movement. Taylor talks of Romanticism emphasising imagination, and its manifestation. He proposes that the very process of manifestation 'helps to define what is to be realised' (p. 374–375). As well as tying action in to the creative impulse, Taylor's conceptualisation of manifestation implies incremental generativity, which I consider to be an important aspect of my model of creativity.

I have been, in this book, attempting to develop a holistic framework of which the rational experience and expression of creativity is just one part. This too might be seen to reflect a Romantic perspective. Thus rather than giving primacy to the rational, to reason and to the conscious, I conceptualise the process of creativity in terms which are holistic, which embrace the non-conscious as well as the conscious, and which include the physical, the emotional and the spiritual.

There are at least three senses, however, in which my proposed holism model differs from the Romantic conception. First, whilst the discovery and expression of feelings were given emphasis during the Romantic period, feelings form only one part of the model I am proposing, as discussed in Chapters 2 and 9.

Second, whilst the source of the creative impulse was conceived of by Romantics as being inward, my model implies the source as being both inward and 'universal'. By acknowledging the unconscious, I conceptualise creativity as having sources both within and beyond the individual, i.e. in the wider 'energy' of the universe. In this sense what I am proposing has something in common with some of the deist approaches to Romanticism, in the work of, for example, Blake, whose works of art were expressions of aspects of God he perceived as manifest in nature and within himself. As Taylor (1989: 377) puts it, 'The artist doesn't imitate nature so much as he imitates the author of nature.' Within the Romantic conception of impulse and expression was the rather Enlightenment-like idea of 'unfoldment', or of there being a natural order which could be 'uncovered'. Yet, my suggestion of universal inspiration for creativity does not imply uncovering but rather construction of ideas.

So a third way in which my holism model differs from the Romantic one is that I do not propose that there is any such Platonic type of order to be discovered, but rather propose an atomistic, chaotic theory of invention.

Creativity, autonomy and pluralism

Another aspect of the Romantic movement which seems reflected within my conception of creativity is the emphasis on the individual (and thus on the particular). As noted in Chapter 1, since my focus is 'little c' rather than 'high' creativity, I acknowledge the individual's creativity rather than that of a wider movement or field of individuals, or indeed the relationship of the individual to that field.

There are, of course, potential social implications of such emphasis on the individual and on the particular. For if the individual's agency is to be evaluated only in relation to the individual and not to a wider field, theory and practice of human action may potentially be driven by this and not by wider, utilitarian or other concerns. Thus ultimately the position of individualism must lead to pluralism in both values and actions which flow from these (indeed as Taylor (1989: 376) points out, one of the cornerstones of the modern – and I would argue too post-modern – political and social life is what he calls 'expressive individuation'). The political consequences of individual creativity have, therefore, something in common with the ideas of the liberal thinker Berlin, as described by Gray (1995).

Earlier in the book, in Chapters 8 and 9, I put forward the proposal that creativity in education requires 'space' and adequate personal autonomy. These ideas seem to have something in common with Berlin's notion of 'negative' freedom which is conceived of as the absence of constraints from others. I have, in this book and elsewhere (Craft, 1996b, 1997), suggested that the rationalism which dominates much teacher development may be inadequate and imbalanced, in that it reflects only a part of human activity and meaning. Again the notion of challenging the rational seems similar to Berlin's challenge to, as Gray (1995: 7) puts it, 'forms of rationalism which have dominated moral and political thought in the English-speaking world over the past century'.

The notion of 'agency' embedded in my notion of creativity reflects Berlin's belief in the supreme ability of the human species to invent, be divergent, find new paths and possibilities. Both my perspective and Berlin's involve a rejection of determinism and a belief in choice, or as Berlin might have it, will (although neither would argue that the exercise of choice is entirely rational or pre-conceived). A presupposition underpinning both is the capacity for choice between alternatives (and, in this sense, to 'invent' the self; as Cooper (1983) has called it, in his discussion of Nietzche's educational philosophy, 'self-creation'). From this perspective flows an acceptance of pluralism of what might be termed 'Goods'.

Summing up: creativity as post-modern virtue

In exploring the political framework or 'Ideal' which surrounds my thinking about creativity, then, I have suggested, so far:

- creativity as a post-modern virtue;
- a broadly Romantic framework for creativity, in terms of the roles ascribed to originality, action, holism, and the emphasis on the individual (although I have highlighted some important distinctions between my current ideas and my understanding of Romantic thinkers' ideas);
- that there are necessary political and social implications of my frame-work for creativity, in that emphasising individuation and agency both demands and produces a liberal and pluralist social order;
- in this sense my ideas have something in common with Berlin's views on negative freedom and consequent values-pluralism, and also with his perspective on holistic 'choice' underpinning individual agency.

In the next part of the chapter, I examine aspects of educating for creativity in a way which fosters humanity.

Education for humanity

As many writers have acknowledged, formal education performs a number of roles in any society; these include a preparation for life beyond school both whilst children are growing up and once they leave the school or education system. Other roles performed by schools include socialisation into social, ethical and political mores and educating for its own sake – inculcating a love of learning.

As suggested in Chapter 10, at this particular point in history it seems timely to consider what kinds of systems are going to be most appropriate for educating in the next century. To identify such systems means acknowledging and aiming to nurture certain, shared, values. I want to propose a primary role for education in fostering values which sustain compassion and humanity between people and their wider environment.

I mean this in several senses. First, as already discussed, acts of creativity, whether 'big c' or 'little c', may work toward both constructive and destructive ends. Thus, it seems to me, one role of education is to encourage children to consider the ethical framework in which acts of creativity take place – both their own and those of others, and to weigh the worth of creativity in the context of these wider values. It may be a creative act to write in permanent marker on an article of clothing which did not have a name label in it, but doing so may have ruined the garment. Similarly, it may be a creative act for an individual child to knock down a collectively built tower, but it is also destroying the work of several people, perhaps without reference to them. I am not suggesting that the appropriate course of action is always clear-cut, but rather that one role of education is to encourage children to consider for themselves what makes an act of creativity appropriate in any given situation.

Second, and leading on from this first example, when fostered without reference to others the creativity of individuals can also expand to crush creativity in others. Thus, for example, encouraging a Y6 child whose literacy skills are very good to write the school end-of-term production is likely to stimulate and help this individual to grow in stature, in a variety of ways. However, other children may find their own creativity as writers, directors, actors, etc. being stifled by the ideas of one person. Similarly, a new game dreamt up by children in the playground which involves a lot of running around may literally take up the space of others wanting a quieter time during their breaks. Fostering the creativity of children means encouraging each child to enter into possibility thinking, in the context of others. This is, of course, as true of adults as it is of children. I have certainly come across the scenario in primary schools where the enthusiasm and creativity of one particular teacher has 'taken over' the professional autonomy and artistry of others. It seems to me that fostering creativity involves fostering also a constant awareness of where creativity 'lands' – how it affects others.

Third, as well as having an impact on other people, children's creativity can have an impact on their immediate and wider physical environment. The new playground game involving much running about may involve flower beds being stampeded. Finding new ways of using the home corner by some children may, if not carefully managed, deny other uses of it to other children. A bright idea about how to tidy up the games cupboard, if not communicated to others, may lead to confusion about where things are kept. Here, my point is that one role which educators take on when fostering creativity is encouraging awareness of and communication with others, entwined with stimulating individual children to ask and follow through on possibility questions such as 'what if?'.

Finally, acts of creativity in the wider world can – and should – be scrutinised by children. A primary role of education in the twenty-first century, more than ever before, must surely be to help children to critically analyse the acts of creativity of others which affect all of our lives. Whole sets of live issues at the moment include the genetic modification of foodstuffs, medical procedures involving interference with the cell structure of living beings, the use of large-scale farming methods, the conflict over land rights in the Middle East and elsewhere, and the construction of an international space station. There are many other examples. All involve a great deal of possibility thinking, all have pros and cons; none is a straightforwardly clear-cut 'good'. We leave this world in our children's hands; they need to be equipped to evaluate the appropriateness of acts of 'high' creativity which will affect them, their children and their grandchildren.

In these several different ways, then, creativity does not necessarily, of itself, involve compassion and humanity. It is a role of education to foster these qualities in children, for without them creativity may be destructive, unhelpful and negative in some ways.

Playing a part in creating the big picture

Some years ago, I stood on a beach in Suffolk in the middle of winter with a question in my mind as to how to proceed with a research project, in which there seemed to be several major lines of enquiry. I was pondering which to follow. As I stood there, battered by the wind and watching the crashing waves pounding and foaming along the smooth shoreline, I realised that the live, moving picture in front of me was enormously wide and deep. It struck me, with some surprise, that the 'big picture' was also a possibility for my research problem.

'Keeping the picture big', it seems to me, is a characteristic of vision. For vision involves holding open many possibilities. I want to propose a way of doing this which involves Bohm and Peat's (1989) notion of 'the implicate' introduced in Chapter 8. My approach starts with individual action, which rejects cynicism and involves practising creative vision in oneself.

Trusting the generative potential of implicate understandings

For each aspect of our lives we have everyday, 'working' theories and explanations. Thus, we may have, for example, our own theories about who has authority in a particular school, or what it is possible to achieve in fostering children's creativity. Such theories are born, largely, of experience: our own and what we have learned about from others. What we take to be the reality of our lives, including the limits to change, is sometimes called 'the explicate world'. It is supported by our working theories of action.

But underneath our explicate world is what Bohm and Peat call an 'implicate world' (1989) – introduced briefly in Chapter 8 of this book. Often more complex than our explicate ones, implicate understandings can be more difficult to articulate; we have perhaps all experienced moments when we are frustrated by being unable to fully explain a complicated idea. Implicate ideas are distinct in another way from explicate ones; they have generative potential. Thus, the flash of understanding which is so hard to explain holds within it many possible unfoldments.

If you visualise how you would like to see transformation occur within the education system, you may find yourself getting stuck. One reason for this may be that the explicate order, the here-and-now, supported by your theories of why it is as it is, has a powerful hold. The here-and-now provides resistance to generative, new possibilities. You may find yourself saying 'Well, I think children should not have to attend school if they don't want to', but then you may find yourself saying 'but who would look after them and how would they learn anything?' Our experience of what we already know provides all kinds of reasons to resist change – and the more complex our experience, the greater our resistance.

Bohm and Peat argue that we need more access to the implicate orders which underlie our explicate ones, because of their generative potential. In this sense they are the source of our creativity. Following through from Bohm and Peat, I would argue that we now need to foster an order of creativity which extends into social organisation, science, culture and consciousness. This means allowing our implicate and generative selves to have a voice, since that is the source of our creative intelligence.

The complexity of the problems which surround society of which our education system forms a part does provide a massive challenge to our creative intelligence. A growing inequitable distribution of wealth within prosperous society, environmental destruction, revolutions in technology, spirituality, management and communications, all bring creative possibilities and also massive uncertainty regarding the nature of existence, work and human action in the world.

As teachers we have a critical role in shaping a vision for educating which responds with compassion to the uncertainty and instability which grows around us.

Individual action in relation to others

Whilst acknowledging the societal barriers and challenges to creativity in education discussed in Chapter 10, and Barber's suggestion that we require 'visionary and assertive leadership' (Barber, 1996: 291), I also believe that individual actions make a difference. And, that as individuals develop so do the institutions of which they are part. But only if we each take our development and our vision in to our workplaces – which means having the courage and the compassion to speak from the heart. This involves awareness of status, among other things.

When learning a new role, actors often play a status game where each player performs his character in high or low status relative to another. Consider, in your own workplace, your perception of your status in relation to each of your colleagues. Consider, too, how you may be perceived by each of them. Finally, consider what possibilities there may be for change in these relationships. For by discerning how you act to maintain an unequal balance, new possibilities may open up for change in the relationship, in order to make your own visions known. Consider what support you might need to make these changes, allowing implicate knowledge to guide you.

Cynicism and its effect on creative action

Cynicism is perhaps the most negating of human activities. Its origin lies deep within our own personal disappointments and needs immediate addressing. Cynicism acts as a punishment on all new ideas, and although ironic and sometimes witty, it can dismantle all sorts of opportunities for transformation, although it is also a source of cultural identification (cynicism provides a source of humour in the British context, although not in the American one).

By recognising the effect of cynicism on our professional lives, it may be possible to open up possible choices for transformation. The following questions were devised by Jana Dugal with this in mind.

> How do I use my cynicism at work?
>
> What language do I use to maintain it?
>
> What is possible when I stop being cynical?
>
> Whose fault is it?
>
> What choices are available to me?
>
> How can I create relationship without blame?
>
> Who do I blame? Avoid? Please? in order to get my own way?
> What, and who, needs forgiving?
>
> What is compassion? How can my compassion speak for me?
> What conversation is possible with compassion?'
>
> (Craft and Dugal, 1997: 113–114)

Dugal describes finding these questions helpful when working in schools where a number of problems had led to immense self-defeat. She cites an example of a school where the Head was isolated and tyrannical, another in which the choices for teachers seemed slim and under-resourced. In each school there was evidence of deep cynical responses as a survival mechanism. Staff and schools alike maintained a policy of mutual hostility. When we recognise we are each accountable for this happening, then we can choose to maintain it, or change. She suggests that the minute we choose a change, all things are possible.

Transformation, through vision, lights up a path out of negativity, often stating that the negative belief is just that – a belief. Recognising this, and acting from a new place of assurance and conviction, leads to transformation.

Practising

Imagine the challenge faced by George:

Having trained to teach infants, George taught the Reception class in an inner London school for two years. When a colleague retired, he had the opportunity to teach children aged 9 and 10. He took up the challenge feeling nervous and ill-equipped. The advice his head teacher gave was, 'Act the part and the rest will follow.' This made little sense to George but he invented a persona and tried it out for the first few weeks. He was a great success with the children who found his blend of high expectations, discipline and warmth both encouraging and stimulating. Years later, when he eventually moved on from that school, children and parents petitioned him to stay. He had successfully blended his pretend persona with his actual one and had learned to act the part of the teacher with authenticity, both to his role and to his own personality.

For some, this may be a familiar story. Practising 'in role' is one way of overcoming fear, blocks and barriers. Having a go is essential to taking creative action. Whatever the outcomes of your own actions to transform children's learning, at whatever level, what will keep you going is the engine phrase, 'what if?'

A similar story is told by Steve, an LEA adviser in one of the Home Counties and an Ofsted Inspector for geography.

> I have responsibility, among other things, for inspecting families who educate at home. A growing number of parents in my LEA are taking this decision. I am concerned at the exhaustion among many teachers whom I meet, and their lack of creative energy. I find myself under constant pressure to 'perform' in my job, as almost all of the services which I provide to schools are now 'bought back' by them. My continued employment therefore depends on how the teachers and schools perceive my worth. As an Ofsted Inspector in schools in my own and other LEAs, I feel concerned at the pressures the experience creates for whole school communities and wonder whether it is appropriate to do this. I feel my heartfelt concerns, to support and inspire teachers and children, are under great pressure. My instinctual reaction is to gradually begin to stand outside the mainstream frame. Step by step, I have begun to introduce in-service courses which address more personal issues for teachers of geography, and I have started to involve myself in a number of national initiatives focusing on vision and creativity in education. Although I still feel these are early days, I am discovering other staff from within the LEA who are involved in these wider initiatives, and who want to create a different vision for their school, their area of responsibility in the LEA, or their own working life. I am practising! I'm starting to say 'what if?' for more and more of my time.

Re-engineering and its impact

Steve's story tells the tale of what Hammer and Champy (1993) call 're-engineering'. Describing the business revolution, they define re-engineering a company as 'tossing aside old systems and starting over. It involves going back to the beginning and inventing a better way of doing work.' As argued in Chapter 10, this is going to be an important notion in reconceptualising what educating could look like in the twenty-first century.

Consider what your own story of re-engineering education could look like; who it is focused on, what are you prepared and able to toss aside at present.

In starting to contemplate this question, you may have become aware of the impact of possibilities on surrounding contexts. For as we re-engineer our ideas in one part of our lives, other aspects are affected. We might, for example, try out a thought-experiment scenario in which schools were used as buildings in which community lifelong learning took place on an individualised basis, in ways similar to those proposed by myself (Craft *et al.*, 1997) or Bentley (1998). Questions immediately arise about the role of technology, the role of the teacher, the resource-flow model, the entitlements and obligations of parents and their children to learning opportunities, the status of the National Curriculum and its assessment arrangements – and there are of course many more. At a smaller level, a thought-experiment involving a Y1 class teacher might focus on organising reading in a way which is more heavily supported by the computer, a local poet who happens to be a willing parent of children at the school, and the local library. The practicalities of introducing this approach may have a variety of impacts in the school as a whole, including the raising of questions about whether other teachers should explore doing something similar, the possibility of improving continuity and progression, the time-tabling of certain activities and of certain support staff, the role of parents in general, etc. All actions, then, are tied in to other parts of the whole – but in re-engineering, the focus is ultimately at the macro-level, in deeply redefining how things are done. The 'ripple effect' of decisions in re-engineeering education, then, is likely to be far reaching.

Attitudes, too, carry over from one aspect of life to others, since our lives are made up of myriad overlapping arenas. Experiencing success or defeat in one part of our life can influence other parts of our lives. What we need to do in overcoming blocks to our creativity is to both analyse the block and synthesise our experience of it with the other segments of our life.

Shallcross (1981) describes a technique for doing this, which involves dividing a sheet of paper into six columns, entitled:

- Role
- Major goal
- Major obstacle
- Usual result
- Desired result
- Alternative behaviour.

In the first column, she suggests writing down all of the roles one is aware of taking on, including both the obvious and the not-so-obvious. In completing the second column, she suggests matching the goals with each role listed, then completing the other columns, except for the last one, by working down or along, whichever seems easier.

She then recommends a consideration of what information the chart reveals to you. In most roles one's major goal has obstacles which are easily overcome. However, for those where the obstacles are problems, some thinking is required. Shallcross suggests for these applying the following questions – and then, if possible, talking answers through with someone who knows you well:

- Is the goal one I have a real investment in?
- Does the same obstacle appear more than once on my chart?
- Is the obstacle to do with my attitudes?
- Is the obstacle external to me?
- Is the obstacle internal to me?
- Is the obstacle real?

Thus, it may be that an obstacle turns out to be non-existent. Or that, another, once noticed, is easily overcome. The final column of the sheet is designed to enable the brainstorming of possible ways of altering one's own behaviour, so that the desired result is forthcoming.

The method proposed by Shallcross is, of course, just one approach. Whatever means one uses to explore obstacles and to consider possible courses of action, what is at work here is the notion of 'possibility'. Ultimately, choosing and trying out a possible behaviour or course of action is essential. And trying out a possible course of action or behaviour in one aspect of your life brings a change in other aspects. It is important to remember, too, that nothing succeeds in giving confidence to behave differently more than actually practising it.

Summing up: creativity, individual action and re-engineering the wider vision

I have suggested that creativity can be used for both constructive and destructive ends and that an important role for education is in fostering critical scrutiny of the implications of creative acts, at the level of both everyday creativity and in considering acts of high creativity.

I have proposed that individual action has an important role to play in harnessing system level vision. I have explored a number of aspects of both fostering and blocking individual action, including the roles played by trusting implicate knowledge, practising and cynicism.

I have suggested that Hammer and Champy's notion of re-engineering, initially designed for a business context, is appropriately applied to education. In looking at the notion of re-engineering I have acknowledged the impact which decisions in one part of one's life may have on other parts.

In the last part of the chapter I want to look at this interconnectedness a little further, exploring the notion of 'humane creativity', a term coined by Professor Howard Gardner.

Humane creativity: a part of the whole

So far, I have suggested in this book that creativity in classrooms needs to be fostered as a part of a whole. This means that the social context for children needs to form part of the background to creating, whatever the object of creation. All children belong to a community, or more likely, several: for example, their family, their school, their neighbourhood, their friendship groups, their religious or spiritual allegiance (if any), their interest groupings (clubs, activities, etc.). Creative acts have a potential impact on this wider social context, which may be overlooked in an individualised market-orientated society. Indeed it is the domination of innovation in the global marketplace which provides one of the foci for Gardner's investigation of humane creativity; creativity with reference to an ethical framework (Gardner, 1998a, 1999) such that the market model does not drive action in every sphere of life. For, he says, 'You can have creativity without wisdom' (1998a: 12). As the philosopher, Warnock, has argued (1994), whilst we lock ourselves into a personal identity which puts the individual and their acts of creation first, then we will tend to limit our responsibility for the consequences of our acts to those cases where we can trace our own single and separate course of action.

How do we develop individuals and communities so that everyone recognises their interdependence to set alongside their independence? This is a question which has exercised philosophers for centuries.

Traditionally, primary schools have involved a great deal of independent working and learning, for both children and their teachers. Studies have suggested that, although it may not be intended as such by teachers, children often learn individually rather than collaboratively or as part of a group (Galton *et al.*, 1980a, 1980b, 1992; Webb, 1993). Other work has shown that children may be communicating with one another during lessons, but that this is often at a very low conceptual level, such as negotiating over resources (Bennett *et al.*, 1984). Development work such as that by Clark (1996) on how to transform the school community to become co-creative to develop truly collaborative group work, and that of groups such as those at Exeter University studying collaboration, still needs to find its way into the practical values of the primary school (Dunne and Bennett, 1990; Bennett and Carre, 1993; Wragg, 1993; Wragg and Brown, 1993; Brown and Wragg, 1993; Wragg and Dunne 1994).

There is a strong sense in which the current education system accepts competition as inevitable and relates its provision to the values and constructs of competition. We may characterise the learning agenda of the current education system as being tailored to a culture of the development of independence as an Ideal.

Implicit in the systems transformation discussed in Chapter 10 is the notion of interdependence, the idea that to some extent we are all dependent upon one another, and thus to a degree 'in relationship'. The extent to which a school really draws upon the relationships within it, in order to foster interdependence between people here and now and over time, however, varies.

It is certainly the case that collaborative and team work is a natural part of some schools' approach to teaching and learning. Examples of co-creative, interdependent learning include designing classroom 'ground rules' at the start of a school year; paired reading; imaginative play; mini-enterprises or simulations; circle time (such as those developed by Murray White, 1991, 1992, 1994a, 1994b, 1995, 1996).

Relationship with the future

Everything we create today has a relationship with what might be in the future. It is by stimulating creativity and imagination that we can consider the impact of what we do today on what might be.

In dialogue with Rupert Sheldrake, Matthew Fox (Sheldrake and Fox, 1996) talks about our tendency to focus on 'text' rather than 'context'. He is talking about our fragmented relationship with the whole of our environment, in all of its elements – physical, emotional, spiritual, social. His metaphor is appropriate because it signals the intellectualist influences on our learning and on our creativity. In fostering children's creativity, we need to remember our relationship as human beings with our environment. The emotional, physical, spiritual and social dimensions of what we create must become a part of what we value in the classroom. Creativity must be humane, must acknowledge the whole. As Gardner has put it, we all need to aim to do 'good work' (1998b).

In the context of humane creativity, I end with a quotation from George Bernard Shaw. It goes like this.

> You see things that are and say 'why?' But I dream things that never were and say, 'Why not?'

Bibliography

Abbott, J. (1998), 'The search for expertise', *The Journal*, London: The 21st Century Learning Initiative

Acker, S. (1995), 'Carry on caring: the work of women teachers', *British Journal of Sociology of Education*, 16(1): 21–36

Ackoff, R. L. (1981), *Creating the Corporate Future*, New York: Wiley

Adams, James L. (1986), *The Care and Feeding of Ideas: A Guide to Encouraging Creativity*, Reading, MA: Addison-Wesley

Adcock, J. (1994), *In Place of Schools: A Novel Plan for the 21st Century*, London: New Education Press

Ahier, J. and Ross, A. (1995), 'Introduction', in Ahier, J. and Ross, A. (eds), *The Social Subjects within the Curriculum*, London: Falmer

Alexander, P. A., Kulikowich, J. M. and Jetton, T. L. (1994), 'The role of subject-matter knowledge and interest in the processing of linear and non-linear texts', *Review of Educational Research*, New York: American Educational Research Association

Alexander, R. (1996), *Other Primary Schools and Ours: Hazards of International Comparisons*, CREPE Occasional Paper, University of Warwick: Centre for Research in Elementary and Primary Education

Amabile, T. (1983), *The Social Psychology of Creativity*, New York: Springer-Verlag

Amabile, T. (1985), 'Motivation and creativity: effects of motivational orientation on creative writers', *Journal of Personality and Social Psychology*, 48: 393–399

Amabile, T. (1990), 'Within you, without you: the social psychology of creativity, and beyond', in Runco, M. A. and Albert, R. S. (eds), *Theories of Creativity*, pp. 61–91, Newbury Park, CA: Sage Publications

Anning, A. (1994), 'Play and legislated curriculum', in Moyles, J. (ed.), *The Excellence of Play*, Buckingham: Open University Press

Armstrong, M. (1980), *Closely Observed Children: Diary of a Primary Classroom*, London: Writers and Readers

Assagioli, R. (1974), *The Act of Will*, London: Wildwood House

Assessment of Performance Unit (APU) (1991), *The Assessment of Performance in Design and Technology*, London: SEAC

Assessment of Performance Unit (APU) (1993), 'Learning Through Design and Technology', in McCormick, R. *et al.*, *Teaching and Learning Technology*, Harlow: Addison Wesley

Avis, J., Bloomer, M., Esland, G. M., Gleeson, D. and Hodkinson, P. (1996), *Knowledge and Nationhood: Education, Politics and Work*, London: Cassell

Banathy, B. H. (1991), *Systems Design of Education; A Journey to Create the Future*, Englewood Cliffs, NJ: Educational Technology Publications Inc.

Banathy, B. H. (1992), 'Systems design: the third culture', *Educational Technology*, XXXII (11), November: 41–46, Englewood Cliffs, NJ: Educational Technology Publications Inc.

Banathy, B. H. (1996), *Designing Social Systems in a Changing World*, New York: Plenum

Barber, M. (1996), *The Learning Game: Arguments for an Education Revolution*, London: Cassell

Barber, M. and Brighouse, T. (1992), *Partners in Change: Enhancing the Teaching Profession*, London: IPPR

Barron, F. (1969), *Creative Person and Creative Process*, New York: Holt, Rinehart and Winston

Barrow, R. (1988), 'Some observations on the concept of imagination', in Egan, K. and Nadaner, D. (eds), *Imagination and Education*, Buckingham: Open University Press

Beetlestone, F. (1998), *Creative Children, Imaginative Teaching*, Buckingham: Open University Press

Belbin, R. Meredith (1981), 'A self-perception inventory' in *Management Teams: Why they Succeed or Fail*, Oxford: Heinemann Professional

Bennett, S. N. and Carre, C. (1993), *Learning to Teach*, London: Routledge

Bennett, N., Desforges, C., Cockburn, A. and Wilkinson, B. (1984), *The Quality of Pupil Learning Experiences*, London: Lawrence Erlbaum Associates

Bentley, T. (1998), *Learning Beyond the Classroom: Educating for a Changing World*, London: Routledge

Best, D. (1990), *Arts in Schools: A Critical Time*, Birmingham Institute of Art and Design, an NSEAD Occasional Publication

Best, D. (1992), *The Rationality of Feeling*, London: Falmer Press

Billen, A. (1996), 'The new age gurus', *Observer Life*, 1 September

Blyth, W. A. L. *et al.* (1976), *Place, Time and Society 8–13: Curriculum Planning in History, Geography and Social Science*, Bristol: Collins/ESL

Boden, M. (1992), *The Creative Mind*, London: Abacus

Bohm, D. and Peat, P. D. (1989), *Science, Order and Creativity*, London: Routledge

Book, C., Byers, J. and Freeman, D. (1983), 'Student expectations and teacher education traditions with which we cannot live', *Journal of Teacher Education*, 34: 30–51

Brierley, J. (1987), *Give me a Child until he is Seven*, Lewis: Falmer

Briggs, M. (1989), 'Perceptions of confidence: an investigation into primary mathematics co-ordinators' perceptions of their colleagues' confidence in teaching mathematics', unpublished dissertation, MA in Curriculum Studies, University of London Institute of Education

Brown, G. and Wragg, E. C. (1993), *Questioning*, London: Routledge

Bruce, T. (1991), *Time to Play in Early Childhood Education*, London: Hodder and Stoughton Educational

Bruce, T. (1994), 'Play, the universe and everything!', in Moyles, J. (ed.), *The Excellence of Play*, Buckingham: Open University Press.

Cameron, J. (1995), *The Artist's Way: A Spiritual Path to Higher Creativity*, London: Pan

Campbell, R. (1985), *Developing the Primary School Curriculum*, London: Holt, Rinehart and Winston

Carr, D. (1991), *Educating the Virtues*, London: Routledge

CBI Education Foundation and the Department for Trade and Industry (1994), *Innovation: Putting Ideas to Work*, London: UBI/Teacher Placement Service

Central Advisory Council for Education (England) (CACE) (1967), *Children and their Primary Schools*, London: Department of Education and Science, HMSO

Clark, D. (1996), *Schools as Learning Communities: Transforming Education*, London: Cassell

Claxton, G. (1984), *Live and Learn: An Introduction to the Psychology of Growth and Change in Everyday Life*, London: Harper and Row

Claxton, G. (1997), *Hare Brain, Tortoise Mind: Why Intelligence Increases When You Think Less*, London: Fourth Estate

Clayden, E., Desforges, C., Mills, C. and Rawson, W. (1994), 'Authentic activity and learning', *British Journal of Educational Studies*, XXXXII (2), June 1994, Oxford/ Cambridge, MA: Blackwell. Later reproduced in Craft, A. (ed.) (1996), *Primary Education: Assessing and Planning Learning*, London: Routledge

Cline, S. (1989), *What Would Happen If I Said Yes? . . .* , New York: D.O.K. Publishers

Cohen, D. and MacKeith, S. A. (1991), *The Development of Imagination: The Private Worlds of Childhood*, London and New York: Routledge

Coleridge, S. T. (1954), *Biographia Literaria*, London: Oxford University Press

Collings, J. A. (1978), 'A psychological study of female specialists in the sixth form', unpublished Ph.D. thesis, University of Bradford

Cooper, David E. (1983), *Authenticity and Learning: Nietzsche's Educational Philosophy*, London: Routledge

Cooper, P. and McIntyre, D. (1996a), *Effective Teaching and Learning: Teachers' and Pupils Perspectives*, Buckingham: Open University Press

Cooper, P. and McIntyre, D. (1996b), 'The importance of power sharing in classroom learning', in Hughes, M. (ed.), *Teaching and Learning in Changing Times*, pp. 88–108, Oxford: Blackwell

Cowie, H. (1989), 'Children as writers', in Hargreaves, D. J. (ed.), *Children and the Arts*, Buckingham: Open University Press

Cowie, H. and Hanrott, H. (1984), 'The writing community: a case study of one junior school class', in Cowie, H. (ed.), *The Development of Children's Imaginative Writing*, London: Croom Helm

Craft, A. (1988), 'A study of imagination', unpublished MA thesis, University of London

Craft, A. (1995), 'Cross-curricular integration and the construction of self', in Ahier, J. and Ross, A. (eds), *The Social Subjects Within the Curriculum: Children's Social Learning in the National Curriculum*, London: Falmer

Craft, A. (1996a), *Continuing Professional Development: A Practical Guide for Teachers and Schools*, London: Routledge

Craft, A. (1996b), 'Nourishing Educator Creativity: A holistic approach to CPD', *British Journal of In-service Education*, 22(3), Autumn: 309–322

Craft, A. (1997), 'Identity and creativity: educating for post-modernism?', *Teacher Development: An International Journal of Teachers' Professional Development*, 1(1): 83–96

Craft, A. (1998), 'Themes in critical and creative thinking', unpublished working paper, November 1998

Craft, A. (1999), 'Creative development in the early years: some implications of policy for practice', *The Curriculum Journal*, 10(1), Spring: 135–150

Craft, A. and Dugal, J. (1997), 'Challenges to vision and creativity', in Craft, A. with Dugal, J., Dyer, G., Jeffrey, B. and Lyons, T., *Can You Teach Creativity?* Nottingham: Education Now

Craft, A. with Dugal, J., Dyer, G., Jeffrey, B. and Lyons, T. (1997), *Can You Teach Creativity?* Nottingham: Education Now

Craft, A. and Lyons, T. (1996), 'Nourishing the educator'. Unpublished seminar paper from The Open University Seminar Network, January

Craft, A., Pain, T. and Shepherd, R. (1996), 'Creativity and Pedagogy in Spain', unpublished working paper, September 1996

Croall, J. (1996), 'Time to explore the hidden depths of your own creativity', *The Times Educational Supplement*, 5 April

Cross, A. (1994), *Design and Technology 5–11*, London: Hodder and Stoughton

Csikszentmihalyi, M. (1988), 'Society, culture and person: a systems view of creativity', in Sternberg, R. J. (ed.), *The Nature of Creativity*, New York: Cambridge University Press

Csikszentmihalyi, M. (1992), *Flow: The Psychology of Happiness*, London: Random House

Csikszentmihalyi, M. (1994), 'The domain of creativity' in Feldman, D. H., Csikszentmihalyi, M. and Gardner, H., *Changing the World: A Framework for the Study of Creativity*, Westport, CT and London: Praeger

Csikszentmihalyi, M. (1996), *Creativity: Flow and the Psychology of Discovery and Invention*, New York: Harper Collins

Cullingford, C. (1991), *The Inner World of the School*, London: Cassell Educational

Dadds, M. (1993), 'The feeling of thinking in professional self-study', *Educational Action Research*, 1(2): 287–303

Dadds, M. (1995) 'Continuing professional development: nurturing the expert within', *Cambridge Institute of Education Newsletter*, 30, Autumn/Winter

Dansky, J. L. (1980), 'Make-believe: a mediator of the relationship between play and associative fluency', *Child Development*, 51: 576–579

de Bono, E. (1967), *The Use of Lateral Thinking*, Harmondsworth: Penguin

de Bono, E. (1995), *Parallel Thinking: From Socratic to de Bono Thinking*, London: Penguin

Delamont, S. and Galton, M. (1987), 'Anxieties and anticipations – pupils' views of transfer to secondary school', in Pollard, A. (ed.), *Children and Their Primary Schools*, London: Falmer Press

Department for Education (1995a), *The National Curriculum (England): Art*, London: DFE/HMSO

Department for Education (1995b), *The National Curriculum: (England) English*, London: DFE/HMSO

Department for Education (1995c), *The National Curriculum (England): Geography*, London: HMSO

Department for Education (1995d), *The National Curriculum (England): History*, London: HMSO

Department for Education (1995e), *The National Curriculum (England): Information Technology*, London: HMSO

Department for Education (1995f), *The National Curriculum (England): Mathematics*, London: DFE/HMSO

Department for Education (1995g), *The National Curriculum (England): Music*, London: DFE/HMSO

Department for Education (1995h), *The National Curriculum (England): Physical Education* London: DFE/HMSO

Department for Education (1995i), *The National Curriculum (England): Science*, London: DFE/HMSO

Design and Technology in Education Project (1990), *What is Design?*, Halifax: Design Dimension Educational Trust

Dunne, E. and Bennett, S. N. (1990), *Talking and Learning in Groups*, London: Routledge

Dyer, G. C. (1995), 'Developing a family declaration of interdependence: a methodology for systems design within a small social unit', *Systems Research*, 12(3): 201–208

Dyer, G. C. and Craft, A. (1997), 'Systems design for education', in Dyer, G. C. with Craft, A. Dugal, J., Jeffrey, B. and Lyons, T., *Can You Teach Creativity?* Nottingham: Education Now

Edwards, A. and Knight, P. (1994), *Effective Early Years Education: Teaching Young Children*, Buckingham: Open University Press

Edwards, G. (1993), *Stepping into the Magic*, London: Piatkus

Edwards, Linda Carol (1990), *Affective Development and the Creative Arts: A Process Approach to Early Childhood Education*, Columbus, OH: Merrill

Edwards, R. (1995), 'Troubled times? Personal identity, distance education and distance learning', unpublished paper

Edwards, R. (1997), 'Knowledge and the Body', unpublished seminar paper from Experiential Research Group, The Open University, April 1997

Egan, K. (1992), *Imagination in Teaching and Learning*, Routledge: London

Elliott, R. K. (1975), *Imagination: A Kind of Magical Faculty*, Inaugural Lecture, University of Birmingham, 1975

Feldman, D. H. (1994), 'Creativity: dreams, insights and transformations', in Feldman, D. H., Csikszentmihalyi, M. and Gardner, H. (1994), *Changing the World: A Framework for the Study of Creativity*, Westport, CT: Praeger

Feldman, D. H., Csikszentmihalyi, M. and Gardner, H. (1994), *Changing the World: A Framework for the Study of Creativity*, Westport, CT, London: Praeger

Fontana, D. (1994), *Growing Together: Parent-Child Relationships as a Path to Wholeness and Happiness*, Shaftesbury: Element Books

Fontana, D. (1997), 'Childhood and an education for being', *Caduceus* Issue 34, Winter 1996/7, Leamington Spa: Caduceus Publications

Freud, A. (1936), *The Ego and the Mechanisms of Defence*, London: Hogarth Press

Freud, S. (1894), *The Neuro-Psychoses of Defence (1): Standard Edition of the Complete Psychological Works of Sigmund Freud, Vol. 3*, London: Hogarth Press and the Institute of Psychoanalysis

Fritz, R., (1943), *The Path of Least Resistance*, Salem, MA: Stillpoint

Fryer, M. (1994), 'Management style and views about creativity', in H. Geschka, S. Moger and T. Rickards (eds), *Creativity and Innovation: The Power of Synergy*, Darmstadt, Germany: Geschka

Fryer, M. (1996), *Creative Teaching and Learning*, London: Paul Chapman

Fryer, M. and Collings, J. A. (1991), 'Teachers' views about creativity', *British Journal of Educational Psychology*, 61: 207–219

Galton, M. (1987), 'An ORACLE chronicle: a decade of classroom research', *Teaching and Teacher Education*, 3: 299–313

Galton, M. and Simon, B. (1980a), *Progress and Performance in the Primary Classroom*, London: Routledge and Kegan Paul

Galton, M., Simon, B. and Croll, P. (1980b), *Inside the Primary Classroom*, London: Routledge and Kegan Paul

Galton, M. and Williamson, J. (1992), *Group Work in the Primary School*, London: Routledge

Gammage, P. (1996), 'Barriers to creativity', Keynote Lecture at Conference on Creativity in Education, June 1996, The Open University, London

Gardner, H. (1983), *Frames of Mind: The Theory of Multiple Intelligences*, London: William Heinemann

Gardner, H. (1993a), *Multiple Intelligences: The Theory in Practice*, New York: HarperCollins

Gardner, H. (1993b), *Creating Minds: An Anatomy of Creativity Seen Through the Lives of Freud, Einstein, Picasso, Stravinsky, Eliot, Graham and Gandhi*, New York: HarperCollins

Gardner, H. (1994), *The Arts and Human Development*, New York: BasicBooks

Gardner, H. (1996), 'Are there additional intelligences? The case for naturalist, spiritual, and existential intelligences', in Kane, J. (ed.), *Education, Information and Transformation*, Engelwood Cliffs, NJ: Prentice-Hall

Gardner, H. (1998a), 'Who does good work?', the Howard Gardner talk to the teachers of the Peconic Teachers' Association, Sag Harbor, 12 March

Gardner, H. (1998b), 'Navigating toward good work', commencement address delivered at Pennsylvania State University, 8 August

Gardner, H. (1999), 'The Vehicle and the vehicles of leadership', *American Behavioural Scientist*, 42(6): 849–863

Garrison, J. (1997), *Dewey and Eros: Wisdom and Desire in the Art of Teaching*, New York: Teachers' College Press

Garvey, C. (1982), *Play*, London: Fontana

Gawain, S. (1978), *Creative Visualization*, San Rafael, CA: New World Library

Gilligan, C. (1982), *In a Different Voice: Psychological Theory and Women's Development*, Cambridge, MA: Harvard University Press

Gilligan, C. (1986), 'Remapping development: the power of divergent data', in Crillo, L. and Wapner, S. (eds), *Value Presupposition in Theories of Human Development*, Hillsdale, NJ: Lawrence Erlbaum Associates

Gilligan, C., Ward, J. V. and Taylor, C. V. (eds) (1988), *Mapping the Moral Domain*, Cambridge, MA: Harvard University Press

Glasser, W. (1992), *The Quality School*, New York: Harper Perennial

Glouberman, D. (1989), *Life Choices and Life Changes Through Imagework: The Art of Developing Personal Vision*, London: Unwin Hyman

Goleman, D. (1996), *Emotional Intelligence: Why it can matter more than IQ*, London: Bloomsbury

Graves, D. (1983), *Writing: Teachers and Children at Work*, Exeter, NH: Heinemann

Gray, J. (1995), *Berlin*, London: Fontana Modern Masters

Halliwell, S. (1993), 'Teacher creativity and teacher education', in Bridges, D. and Kerry, T. (eds), *Developing Teachers Professionally*, London and New York: Routledge

Hammer, M. and Champy, J. (1993), *Re-engineering the Corporation: Manifesto for a Business Revolution*, London: Brearley Publishing

Hammond, J. H. (1988), 'The second wave: information technology and literacy', in Sendov, A. B. and Stanchev, I. (eds), *Children in the Information Age: Opportunities for Creativity, Innovation and New Activities, Selected Papers from the Second International Conference, Sofia, Bulgaria 19–23 May 1987*, Oxford: Pergamon Press

Handy, C. (1994), *The Empty Raincoat: Making Sense of the Future*, London: Hutchinson

Hardie, W. R. F. (1980), *Aristotle's Ethical Theory*, Oxford: Clarendon Press

Hargreaves, A. (1994), *Changing Teachers, Changing Times*, London: Cassell

Hargreaves, A. and Tucker, E. (1991), 'Teaching and guilt: exploring the feelings of teaching', *Teaching and Teacher Education*, 7(5/6): 491–505

Hargreaves, D. H., Galton, M. J. and Robinson, S. (1989), 'Developmental psychology and arts education', in Hargreaves, D. J. (ed.), *Children and the Arts*, Buckingham: Open University Press

Hargreaves, Linda M. and Hargreaves, David J. (1997), 'Children's development 3–7: the learning relationship in the early years', in Kitson, N. and Merry, R. (eds), *Teaching in the Primary School: A Learning Relationship*, London: Routledge

Haylock, D. and Cockburn, A. (1989), *Understanding Early Years Mathematics*, London: Paul Chapman

Hegelson, S. (1990), *The Female Advantage: Women's Ways of Leadership*, New York: Doubleday

Holly, M. L. (1989), *Writing to Grow: Keeping a Personal-Professional Journal*, Portsmouth, NH: Heinemann

Holt, J. (1991), *Learning all the Time*, Nottingham: Education Now Publishing Co-operative, in association with Lighthouse Books

Holt, J. (1992), *Never Too Late*, Ticknall: Education Now

Honey, P. and Mumford, A. (1986), *A Manual of Learning Styles*, Maidenhead: Peter Honey and Alan Mumford

Hudson, L. (1973), *Originality*, London: Oxford University Press

Hurst, V. (1997), *Planning for Early learning: Educating Young Children*, London: PCP

Institute for Creativity (1995), 'Creativity in Education: Holistic Postgraduate Course for Educators', taught from October 1995 to May 1996, London: Institute for Creativity

Jackson, J. R. de J., (1969), *Method and Imagination in Coleridge's Criticism*, London: Routledge and Kegan Paul

Jackson, M. (1987), 'Making sense of school', in Pollard, A. (ed.), *Children and Their Primary Schools*, London: Falmer Press

Jeffrey, B. (1997), 'Framing creativity in primary classrooms', in Craft, A., with Dugal, J., Dyer, G., Jeffrey, B. and Lyons, T., *Can You Teach Creativity?* Nottingham: Education Now

Jeffrey, B. and Woods, P. (1997), 'The relevance of creative teaching: pupils' views' , in Pollard, A., Thiessen, D. and Filer, A., *Children and Their Curriculum: The Perspectives of Primary and Elementary School Children*, London: Falmer Press

Jeffrey, B. and Woods, P. (1998), *Testing Teachers*, London: Falmer Press

Jung, C. J. (1995), *Memories, Dreams and Reflections* (recorded and edited by Aniela Jaffe, translated from the German by Richard and Clara Winston), London: Fontana (originally published in German under the title *Erinnerungen, Tauma, Gedanken*, copyright held by Random House Inc. 1961)

Kellner, D. (1992), 'Popular culture and the construction of postmodern identities', in Lash, S. and Friedman, J. (eds), *Modernity and Identity*, Oxford: Basil Blackwell

Kenny, A. (1989), *The Metaphysics of Mind*, Oxford: Oxford University Press

Kimberley, C. (1996), 'Making the impossible possible', in Craft, A. (ed.), *Conference Proceedings: Creativity in Education Conference*, held in London, June 1996, Milton Keynes: Open University

Kirton, M. (ed.) (1989, 2nd edition), *Adaptors and Innovators: Styles of Creativity and Problem Solving*, London: Routledge

Lazarus, M. (1883) *About the Attraction of Play*, Berlin: Dummler

Lieberman, J. Nina (1977), *Playfulness: Its Relationship to Imagination and Creativity*, New York: Academic Press

Little, J. W. (1996), 'The emotional contours and career trajectories of (disappointed) reform enthusiasts', *Cambridge Journal of Education*, 26(3): 345–360

Loveless, A. (1995), *The Role of I.T.: Practical Issues for the Primary Teacher*, London: Cassell

McCormick, R. (1998), 'Learning schools programme: an outline', Milton Keynes: Open University Project Briefing Paper

McCormick, R. and Davidson, M. (1996), 'Problem solving and the tyranny of product outcomes', *Journal of Design and Technology Education*, 1 (3): 230–241

MacKinnon, D. W. (1962) 'What makes a person creative?' *Saturday Review*, 10 February

MacKinnon, D. W. (1978), *In Search of Human Effectiveness: Identifying and Developing Creativity*, Buffalo, NY: Creative Education Foundation, and Great Neck, NY: Creative Synergetic Associates

McWilliam, E. (1996), 'Admitting impediments: or things to do with bodies in the classroom', *Cambridge Journal of Education*, 26(3) November: 367–378

Maslow, A. H. (1971), *The Farther Reaches of Human Nature*, Harmondsworth: Penguin

Maslow, A. H. (1987), *Motivation and Personality*, New York and Cambridge: Harper and Row

Meighan, R. (1994), *The Freethinkers' Guide to the Educational Universe*, Nottingham: Educational Heretics Press

Meighan, R. (1995), 'Home-based education effectiveness research and some of its implications', *Educational Review*, 47(3): 275–287

Meighan, R. (1997), *The Next Learning System*, Nottingham: Educational Heretics Press

Millar, S. (1968), *The Psychology of Play*, London: Penguin

Minkin, L. (1997), *Exits and Entrances: Political Research as a Creative Art*, Sheffield: Sheffield Hallam University

Morton, M. (1980), *Frames of Mind: Constraints on the Common-Sense Conception of the Mental*, Oxford: Clarendon Press

Moyles, J. (1989), *Just Playing? The Role and Status of Play in Early Childhood Education*, Buckingham: Open University Press.

Moyles, J. (1997), 'Just for fun? The child as active learner and meaning maker', in Kitson, N. and Merry, R. (eds), *Teaching in the Primary School: A Learning Relationship*, London: Routledge

Moyles, J. R. (ed.) (1994), *The Excellence of Play*, Buckingham: Open University Press

Murphy, P. and Scanlon, E. (1994), *PGCE Teaching in Primary Schools: Primary Science Module 1*, Milton Keynes: Open University

National Advisory Committee on Creative and Cultural Education (1999), *All Our Futures: Creativity, Culture and Education*, London: DSEE

National Commission on Education (1995), *Learning to Succeed: A Radical Look at Education Today and a Strategy for the Future – a Follow-up Report*, London: NCE

National Grid for Learning (1998), *Open for Learning, Open for Business*, London: DfEE

Nias, J. (1989), *Primary Teachers Talking*, London: Routledge and Kegan Paul

Nias, J. (1996), 'Thinking about feeling', *Cambridge Journal of Education*, 26(3): 293–306

Office for Standards in Education (Ofsted) (March, 1996), *Training Course for Registered Nursery Education Inspectors: A Guide for Inspectors*, London: HMSO

Ogden, T. H. (1982), *Projective Identification and Psychotherapeutic Technique*, New York: Jason Aronson

Passmore, J. (1980), *The Philosophy of Teaching*, London: Duckworth

Pepler, D. J. (1982), 'Play and divergent thinking', in Pepler, D. J. and Rubin, K. H. (eds), *The Play of Children: Current Theory and Research*, London: S. Karger

Perkins, David N. (1995), 'Insight in minds and genes', in Sternberg, R. J. and Davidson, J. E.(1995), *The Nature of Insight*, Cambridge, MA: MIT Press

Perkins, David N. (1997), 'Insight in minds and genes', keynote address at 7th International Conference on Thinking, Singapore, June 1997

Perkins, D., Jay, E. and Tishman, S. (1993), 'Beyond abilities: a dispositional theory of thinking, *Merril-Palmer Quarterly*, 39(1): January, 1–21, Detroit, MI: Wayne State University Press

Pintrich, P. R., Marx, R. W. and Boyle, R. A. (1993), 'Beyond cold conceptual change: the role of motivational beliefs and classroom contextual factors in the process of conceptual change', *Review of Educational Research*, Summer, 63(2): 167–199

Pollard, A. (1985), *The Social World of the Primary School*, London: Cassell Education

Pollard, A. (1987), 'Goodies, jokers and gangs', in Pollard, A. (ed.), *Children and Their Primary Schools*, London: Falmer Press

Pollard, A. (1990), *Learning in Primary Schools*, London: Cassell

Pollard, A., Broadfoot, P., Croll, P., Osborne, M. and Abbott, D. (1994), *Changing English Primary Schools? The Impact of the Education Reform Act at Key Stage One*, London: Cassell

la Porte, E. (1996), 'Teaching: getting it right', *Cambridge Journal of Education*, 20(3): 361–366

Redfield, J. (1994), *The Celestine Prophecy*, London: Bantam

Revell, R. (1996), 'Realities and feelings in the work of primary heads', *Cambridge Journal of Education*, 26(3): 391–400

Ritchie, R. (1995), *Primary Design and Technology: A Process for Learning*, London: David Fulton Publishers

Ritzer, G. (1993), *The McDonaldization of Society: An Investigation into the Changing Character of Contemporary Social Life*, Newbury Park, CA: Pine Forge Press

Robinson, K., Wills, G., Allen, D., Henderson, J. and Everitt, P. (1990a), *National Curriculum Council Arts in Schools Project: Practice and Innovation*, Harlow: Oliver and Boyd

Robinson, K., Wills, G., Allen, D., Henderson, J. and Everitt, P. (1990b), *National Curriculum Council Arts in Schools Project: A Curriculum Framework*, Harlow: Oliver and Boyd

Rogers, C. R. (1970), 'Towards a theory of creativity', in Vernon, P. E. (ed.), *Creativity*, Harmondsworth: Penguin

Rogoff, B. (1990), *Apprenticeship in Thinking: Cognitive Development in Social Context*, New York: Oxford University Press

Roney-Dougal, S. (1994), *Where Science and Magic Meet*, Shaftesbury, Element Books

Rosen, B. C., Crockett, H. T. and Nunn, C. Z. (eds) (1969), *Achievement in American Society*, Cambridge, MA: Schenkman

Ross, D., Ackrill, J. L. and Urmson, J. O. (translators and revisors) (1980), *Aristotle: The Nicomachean Ethics*, Oxford: Oxford University Press

Ross, M. (1978), *The Creative Arts*, London: Heinemann Educational

Rowlands, S. (1984), *The Enquiring Classroom*, London: Falmer Press

Ryle, G. (1949), *The Concept of Mind*, London: Hutchinson

Salzberger-Wittenberg, I., Henry, G. and Osborne, E. (1983), *The Emotional Experience of Teaching and Learning*, London: Routledge and Kegan Paul

SCAA (1997), *Looking at Children's Learning: Desirable Outcomes for Children's Learning on Entering Compulsory Education*, London: School Curriculum and Assessment Authority

Scaife, J. and Wellington, J. (1993), *Information Technology in Science and Technology Education*, Buckingham and Philadelphia: Open University Press

Scarlett, G. and Wolf, D. (1979), 'When it's only make-believe: the construction of a boundary between fantasy and reality in story-telling', in Gardner, H. and Winner, E. (eds), *Facts, Fiction and Fantasy in Childhood*, San Francisco: Jossey-Bass

Schaller, J. (1861), *Das Spiel und die Spiele*, Weimar: Bohlan

Schools Examination and Assessment Council (SEAC) (1991), *The Assessment of Performance in Design and Technology (Goldsmith's Project)*, London: HMSO

Scruton, R. (1974), *Art and Imagination: A Study in the Philosophy of Mind*, London: Methuen

Segal, H. (1964), *Introduction to the Work of Melanie Klein*, London: Heinemann

Shagoury Hubbard, R. (1996), *Workshop of the Possible: Nurturing Children's Creative Development*, York, Maine: Stenhouse Publishers

Shallcross, D. J. (1981), *Teaching Creative Behaviour: How to Teach Creativity to Children of All Ages*, Englewood Cliffs, NJ: Prentice-Hall

Sheldrake, R. and Fox, M. (1996), *Natural Grace: Dialogues on Science and Spirituality*, London: Bloomsbury

Singer, J. L. and Singer, D. (1977), 'The values of the imagination', in Sutton, B. (ed.), *Play and Learning*, New York: Gardner Press

Siraj-Blatchford, J. (1996), *Learning Technology, Science and Social Justice: An Integrated Approach for 3–13 Year Olds, An Education Now Handbook*, Nottingham: Education Now Publishing Co-operative

Skinner, P. (1996), 'Innovation and creativity: education and the future of work', Keynote Lecture at Conference on Creativity in Education, June 1996, The Open University, London

Sluckin, A. (1987), 'The culture of the primary school playground', in Pollard, A. (ed.), *Children and their Primary Schools*, London: Falmer

Smart, B. (1993), *Postmodernity*, London: Routledge

Spender, D. (1995), *Nattering on the Net*, Melbourne, Australia: Spinifex Press

Stern, S. (1992), 'The relationship between human resource development, development and corporate creativity in Japan', *Human Resource Development Quarterly*, 3(3), Fall

Sternberg, R. J. and Lubart, Todd I. (1995), 'An investment perspective on creative insight', in Sternberg, R. J. and Davidson, J. E. (1995), *The Nature of Insight*, Cambridge, MA: MIT Press

Tambling, P. (1990), *Performing Arts in the Primary School*, Oxford: Blackwell

Taylor, C. (1989), *Sources of the Self: The Making of the Modern Identity*, Cambridge: Cambridge University Press

Taylor, R. and Andrews, G. (1993) *The Arts in the Primary School*, London: Falmer Press

TTA (Teacher Training Agency) (1998), *National Standards for Subject Leaders*, London: TTA

Teaching as a Career (TASC) (1994a), *Secondary Teaching: The Challenge and the Reward*, London: Department for Education

Teaching as a Career (TASC) (1994b), *My Teacher: Training to Teach in Primary Schools*, London: Department for Education

Thomas, A. (1992), 'Individualised teaching', *Oxford Review of Education*, 18(1): 59–74

Thomas, A. (1994a), 'Conversational learning', *Oxford Review of Education*, 20(1): 131–142

Thomas, A. (1994b), 'The quality of learning experienced by children who are educated at home', presentation given at British Psychological Society Annual Conference, Brighton

Thomas, A. (1998), *Educating Children at Home*, London: Cassell

Tickle, L. (ed.) (1990), *Design and Technology in Primary School Classrooms*, Lewes: Falmer Press

Tizard, B. and Hughes, M. (1984), *Children Learning at Home and in School*, London: Fontana

Tobin, B. (1989), 'An Aristotelian theory of moral development', *Journal of Philosophy of Education*, 23(2): 195–211

Torrance, E. P. (1984), *Mentor Relationships: How they aid Creative Achievement, Endure, Change and Die*, Buffalo, NY: Bearly

Tower, R. B. and Singer, J. L. (1980), 'Imagination, interest and joy in early childhood', in McGhee, P. E. and Chapman, A. J. (eds), *Children's Humour*, Chichester: Wiley

Turkle, S. and Papert, S. (1990), 'Epistemological pluralism: signs and voices within the computer culture', *Signs: Journal of Women in Culture and Society*, 16 (1)

Wallach, M. (1971), *The Creativity-Intelligence Distinction*, New York: General Learning Press

Wallach, M. (1985), 'Creativity testing and giftedness', in Horowitz, F. and O'Brien, M. (eds), *The Gifted and Talented: Developmental Perspectives*, pp. 99–132, Washington, DC: American Psychological Association

Walters, J., Plasket, J., Andrews, B., Powell, K. and Moskowitz, J. (1996), *Research on the Programs of the Aesthetic Education Institutes: The Final Report to the Lincoln Center Institute*, Cambridge, MA: Harvard University Project Zero

Ward, Thomas B., Finke, Ronald A., and Smith, Steven M. (1995), *Creativity and the Mind: Discovering the Genius Within*, New York and London: Plenum Press

Warnock, M. (1976), *Imagination*, London: Faber and Faber

Warnock, M. (1977), *Schools of Thought*, London: Faber and Faber

Warnock, M. (1994), *Imagination and Time*, Oxford: Blackwell.

Webb, R. (1993), *Eating the Elephant Bit by Bit: The National Curriculum at Key Stage 1 and 2: Final report of research commissioned by the Association of Teachers and Lecturers (ATL)*, London: ATL

Wells, G. (1987), *The Meaning Makers*, Sevenoaks: Hodder and Stoughton

West, T. (1991), *In the Mind's Eye: Visual Thinkers, Gifted People with Learning Difficulties, Computer Images, and the Ironies of Creativity*, Amherst, NY: Prometheus, seventh printing, July 1996

White, J. P. (1972), 'Creativity and education: a philosophical analysis', in Dearden, R., Hirst, P. and Peters, R. S., *Education Development and Reason*, London and Boston: Routledge and Kegan Paul

White, J. P (1998), *Do Howard Gardner's Multiple Intelligences add up? Perspectives on Education Policy*, London: Institute of Education University of London

White, M. (1991), *The Benefits of Circle Time*, a 28 page booklet available for £ 4.50 from Murray White, 5 Ferry Path Road, Cambridge, CB4 1HB

White, M. (1992), *Self-Esteem, its Meaning and Value in Schools: A Step by Step Guide to conducting Circle Time in the Classroom*, Packs A and B, Dunstable: Folens

White, M. (1994a), *Raising Self-Esteem: 50 Activities*, Dunstable: Folens

White, M. (1994b), *Picture This: Guided Imagery for Circle Times*, Dunstable: Folens

White, M. (ed.) (1995), *Self-Esteem Solutions*, Dunstable: Folens

White, M. (1996), 'Circle time – What it is, how it works and why children love it', in

Proceedings of the 1996 Creativity in Education Conference, Open University (available from Anna Craft, The Open University School of Education, Walton Hall, Milton Keynes, MK7 6AA)

Wilkinson, A., Barnsley, G., Hannah, P. and Swan, M. (1980), *Assessing Language Development*, Oxford: Oxford University Press

Wilkinson, E. and Willoughby, L. A. (eds and trans.) (1967), *On the Aesthetic Education of Man* by F. von Schiller, Oxford: Oxford Univesrity Press.

Winnicott, D. W. (1971), *Playing and Reality*, New York: Routledge.

Wood, E. and Atfield, J. (1996), *Play, Learning and the Early Childhood Curriculum*, London: PCP

Woods, P. (1990), *Teacher Skills and Strategies*, Lewes: Falmer Press

Woods, P. (1993), *Critical Events in Teaching and Learning*, London: Falmer Press

Woods, P. (1995), *Creative Teachers in Primary Schools*, Buckingham: Open University Press

Woods, P. and Jeffrey, R. (1996), *Teachable Moments*, Buckingham: Open University Press

Wragg, E. C. (1993), *Primary Teaching Skills*, London: Routledge

Wragg, E. C. and Brown, G. (1993), *Explaining*, London: Routledge

Wragg, E. C. and Dunne, R. (1994), *Effective Teaching*, London: Routledge

Zdenek, M. (1985), *The Right-Brain Experience*, London: Corgi

Index